BIG TREES
of NEW HAMPSHIRE

Short Hikes *to the* Biggest Trees *in* New Hampshire
from the Seacoast *to the* North Country

"We 'big tree people' have needed a guide like this for the general public for a long time. Kevin's well-written book presents a wide variety of trees accompanied by beautiful pictures, descriptions to go with them, and location information so **anyone can plan an expedition to hunt for our giants**."

—Carolyn Page, NH Big Tree Program Coordinator

"Big Trees of New Hampshire **will inspire families** to visit and see some of the most spectacular trees in the state. Kevin Martin knows trees from his work as a master wooden boat builder. The book is well illustrated with photos and maps and is organized by tour, from the Seacoast to the North Country. Sidebars explain how big trees are measured, aged and cared for. **This is a must have guide** to learning more about the trees that make New Hampshire the second most forested state in the country. Perhaps along the way you will even find some bigger trees."

—David Govatski is a retired US Forest Service forester and silviculturist from Jefferson, NH.

"This is a great guide to leave in your car for easy reference. If you find yourself with some extra time in an urban area or on a back road in a rural area **Kevin's clear maps and simple descriptions will help you find the big trees**, plus enjoy some beautiful parts of New Hampshire.

Great excursions for visiting family or overseas lumber customers who love to see our forests."

—Jameson French, President, Northland Forest Products

"With 80 years of caring for New Hampshire's trees, we proudly support our fellow tree preservationist, Kevin Martin, in producing this beautiful book **celebrating the diversity and uniqueness of some of New Hampshire's most majestic big trees**."

—New Hampshire Arborists Association, nharborists.org

"The Lamprey Rivers Advisory Committee was thrilled to help Kevin Martin shares his passion for nature and the Big Trees that live among us through *Big Trees of New Hampshire* and *Big Trees of the Lamprey River*. ...His careful guidance to find and appreciate these giants is **a gift to everyone who cares about the special natural heritage of New Hampshire**."

—Lamprey Rivers Advisory Committee

1. Shagbark Hickory
2. White Ash
3. A Wild and Scenic River Big Tree Tour
4. Red Pine
5. Black Tupelo
6. Eastern Hophornbeam
7. Nashua Big Tree Tour
8. Mockernut Hickory
9. Atlantic White Cedar
10. Portsmouth Big Tree Tour
11. Douglas Fir
12. Kingman Farm
13. Eastern White Pine Tours
14. Berlin Test Nursery
15. Snyder Brook
16. Yellow Birch
17. Forest Lake State Park
18. Northern White Cedar
19. Black Spruce
20. Pondicherry National Wildlife Refuge
21. Mountain Paper Birch
22. Fox State Forest
23. Vincent State Forest
24. Connecticut River Valley Oaks
25. Concord Tree Tour
26. Pitch Pine
27. Butternut
28. White Oak

BIG TREES
of NEW HAMPSHIRE

Short Hikes *to the* Biggest Trees *in* New Hampshire
from the Seacoast *to the* North Country

by KEVIN MARTIN

Peter E. Randall Publisher
Portsmouth, New Hampshire
2014

ISBN: 978-1-937721-18-3
Library of Congress Control Number: 2014931985

Published by
Peter E. Randall Publisher
Box 4726
Portsmouth, NH 03802
www.perpublisher.com

Book design: Grace Peirce

Additional copies available from:
Kevin Martin
16 Windsor Lane
Epping, NH 03042
e-mail: kevinmartin16@comcast.net
phone: (603) 679-5153

Maps in this book are courtesy of NH Granit, New Hampshire's
Statewide GIS Clearinghouse, University of New Hampshire Complex
Systems Research Center, Institute for the Study of Earth, Oceans and
Space, on the Web at: www.granit.unh.edu, and granitview.unh.edu

Photographs by Kevin Martin unless otherwise noted.

Contents

Western New Hampshire

Central New Hampshire

Acknowledgments

As a member of the NH Big Tree Program I was lucky to have access to their extensive database of the biggest trees in the state. Many of the volunteers with the program helped by suggesting trees in their area that could be included in the book and also helped in the editing process. I would like to especially thank Sam Stoddard of Lancaster for bringing me along to see the trees up in Coos county and his extensive efforts to supply accurate GPS locations for the trees in this book and all the other trees listed in the state. Carolyn Page and Mary Tebo Davis helped with my many questions and along with Mary Jane Sheldon, do most of the hard work that keeps the Big Tree Program going. County coordinators Kamal Nath, Paul Galloway and Anne Krantz were helpful by directing me to trees in Carroll, Cheshire, and Hillsborough counties.

The state foresters in New Hampshire know where most of the big trees are located and were happy to help with any questions that I had. I would like to thank Fred Borman for getting me going by helping me measure the first few trees that I found. Steve Eisenhaure brought me to some champion trees on UNH land and Ken Desmarais, the current expert in New Hampshire on larch varieties, pointed out their features at Fox and Vincent State Forests.

Retired U.S. Forest Service forester Dave Govatski showed off the trees on the Pondicherry National Wildlife Refuge and pointed out how to recognize some of the northern species that I was not familiar with.

Of course I will thank my family who put up with my obsession for these trees and even let me show them some. My grandchildren happily posed at several trees for pictures when asked. Last I thank my wife Kim, who went along with me to find and measure several trees and did not mind too much when I wandered off the hiking trails or the highways to look at a possible champion that seemed to be nearby on most every trip we took.

Sponsors

The sponsors listed here recognized the value of showing off our Big Trees to the general public who may not have been able to see them otherwise. The primary sponsors include the Lamprey River Advisory Committee who oversees the National Wild and Scenic portion of the Lamprey River. Several trees are listed as a tour of the Lamprey in this book and a separate guide is available through the committee. The New Hampshire Arborists Association, whose members are active in keeping the big trees in our cities and towns in good condition and Northland Forest Products, a lumber distributor and retailer that supports good forestry practices and is a leader in sustainable harvesting in the state.

Support also came from the Nashua Historical Society and the New Hampshire Big Tree Program.

NORTHLAND
FOREST PRODUCTS

Introduction

We all seem attracted to large trees, especially when they are deep in the forest and stand out among the smaller trees near them. If it is a tall tree, the trunk goes up and up and we strain to see the top, while shorter ones can have stout lower branches that look like regular-size trees growing sideways out of the trunk. It feels like a different world when we're under the tree and looking out from the space that is carved out by its limbs. Up close, the bark is more noticeable, and we're drawn in to examine it. There are likely signs of the wildlife, both large and small, that are also drawn in to the shelter provided around the roots and in the tree itself.

Most locals who use the woods know where we are directing them when we say "over by the big oak." We can sit under the tree and let our mind wander, feeling protected by this old forest landmark that has had generations of landowners, hunters, fishermen, and hikers stop for a while to ease the stress of their busy lives.

This book will direct you to an assortment of large trees in New Hampshire that take a hike to get to. I've included trees from all parts of the state so you can travel to different types of forests and see new things on the way. The North Country has its tamarack, spruce-fir, and northern white cedar forests that are in the farthest and wildest reaches of the state. The mountains and south to the Lakes region have a mix of the northern forests species such as tamarack and fir along with the more southerly oaks and pines. The seacoast and western part of the state have the oak, pine, and hickory woods that I know best.

These trips will take you into deep swamps, along river edges and floodplains, up into mountains, and down to the salt marshes near the ocean. The cities and towns of the state have many of the largest Big Trees because they are well cared for, have plenty of sunlight, and little or no competition from other trees. Some of the trips in this book are into these cities or towns where there are several trees that you can walk or bike to and view from the sidewalks.

In today's society with computers and so many other distractions bringing us inside and out of the elements, it is important to be reminded of the natural world around us. These large trees do so much to keep our world in balance. They help control flooding by absorbing water and preventing erosion during heavy rains. They absorb much of the carbon we introduce into the air and give us the oxygen we breathe. We use them in many ways, such as building and furnishing our homes, as a source of heat, and even to cure our illnesses. Viewing these large trees will help us appreciate the tremendous work they do. This book showcases different types of the Big Trees—and sometimes more than one impressive example of the more common ones—so you can learn to identify them.

Although this guidebook is up to date as of 2013, keep in mind that the Big Tree Champions list is always changing. While I was writing this book, the Big Tree Program in New Hampshire was updating the list with some trees that had not been re-measured since the 1970s. Some of the trees listed could not be found because the old directions were lacking in details or the surroundings have changed so much that the landmarks are no longer there. As these trees are found, or new discoveries are added, the list is updated. A common occurrence when searching them out is that the tree has been cut, blown over, or just died and rotted from old age. I have learned not to be too discouraged when finding trees like this. Another younger tree is always willing to try to reach the grand stature that the old giant had attained.

Some of the hikes in this book include trees that are not state or county champions, although they may have been at one time until a larger one was found and the former champ moved down on the list. They are still impressive trees and include an interesting hike to get to them. I hope you enjoy these trips, and be sure to look around while out in the woods of New Hampshire!

What You Will Need to Bring

You can carry a small daypack to hold all of the following.

- Map of area
- Compass
- Tree identification book
- GPS, needed to find some of the trees
- Extra batteries for the GPS
- Insect repellent
- Water
- Snacks
- Camera
- Small first aid kit

Optional items:

- Binoculars
- Tree measuring gear, if desired
- Boots, for wet areas
- Headlamp or flashlight (with extra batteries)
- Warm clothing, hat, and gloves, if needed
- Rain gear, if needed

For the longer hikes, you should bring the items you would normally take hiking. I keep a pack ready with necessities for just such hikes. Even some of the shorter hikes are in woods that are hard to get around in. For those hikes you should be prepared with a GPS (with extra batteries) and a map and compass for backup. During hunting season be sure to wear some hunters' orange clothing to be safe.

Always respect the property you are on and the trees you are viewing. Do not let the kids pull off the bark or hack away at the trunk with whatever they have in hand. Tread softly around the tree so you will not damage any exposed roots.

Some trees are on private property, which could be posted at any time if the owners change or the land is abused. If the land is posted, move on to see another tree. If in a city and the property owners are kind enough to let us view the tree, be kind enough to respect their privacy and do not hang around the front of their house too long. If they want to, they will come to you and tell you about the tree, but they may not want too many people asking a lot of questions.

Even trees on public land will be protected if they're abused, and steps could be taken to restrict viewing them. Just use some common sense so that our children will be able to bring their children back to see these trees in the future.

Trip Difficulty Rating

These descriptions will help you determine what kind of walk you are in for.

1. Short, easy walk with little to no rise in elevation. Good for young families.

2. Moderate walk with some elevation gain, and rocks and roots on the trail. May be a half-mile or more to the tree, and may include additional hiking if desired. Children will still enjoy this.

3. A harder walk that may take some time to get to the area of the tree and then find it. Some off trail travel may be required. Could include wet areas to get through or some elevation gain up steep slopes. Older children with fair hiking skills and the proper equipment will enjoy the challenge.

It can be difficult to get close to an Atlantic White Cedar.

4. An adventure for the experienced hiker; mostly off trail. Expect swamp tromping and bushwhacking. Will take considerable time to get to the tree and then find your way out. Plan on spending half a day, and go early so you are not trying to find your way out in the dark.

Note: Keep in mind that the GPS coordinates have been supplied for the trees, but for some of the trips you will have to mark the coordinates for the access point so you can find your way back out of the woods. Take a compass reading too. Who knows, you could lose your GPS power or signal and will have to depend on a map and compass.

DISCLAIMER

Please be aware of the weather and where you are going in the woods. It is up to you to have all the required equipment. Double-check the GPS readings for any long trips. We cannot be responsible for errors in this book. Trails and conditions can change, so please be aware that this book is but a guide. Respect the forest and enjoy these Big Trees.

About the New Hampshire Big Tree Program

The New Hampshire Big Tree Program is part of a national program that is run in each state to keep track of the largest trees in the states and the country. There are set guidelines on how to measure the trees, with trees re-measured every ten years in order to keep their champion status. County, state, and national champion trees are listed. In New Hampshire, under the best circumstances each county has a team that measures any trees reported. The state coordinator sends out certificates to the landowners and nominators and reports to the national group at American Forests.

How to Measure the Trees

After some time you learn how to spot the big trees and where to look for them in the woods. Edges of clearings and along property boundaries or stonewalls are good places to start. I look down low for large trunks or, in the winter, high up for wide crowns some distance off. Crowns are harder to see in the summer, and you have to be closer because the trees around them have leafed out. Sometimes you just have to wander in an area where you have been told about a certain tree. It may be in the next hundred feet along the trail or around the next bend in the stream.

Once a new tree is found, you should measure it to compare it to others on the list. You need a 25-foot flexible tape measure to check the circumference of the trunk; measure it 4½ feet up, or about breast height, from the ground. If the ground at the trunk is sloped, measure from between the high and low spot up 4½ feet and then around the trunk. That measurement is the circumference breast height, or CBH. You can compare the circumference to others by looking at the NH Big Tree Program website and look up the tree listings there. If you find a tree that's a potential candidate, you can call in a measuring team, and they can compare the size of this tree to other champions on the list.

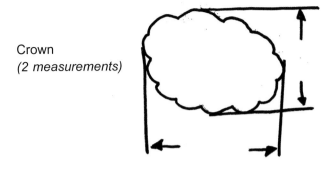

Crown
(2 measurements)

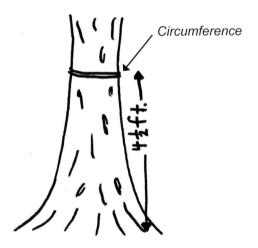

Circumference

The measuring team will recheck the circumference. Then, with a 100-foot tape, they will measure the crown (how wide the branches spread out from the tree) at the widest point, and then take another crown measurement at a right angle to the first one. The crown sizes are added together and divided by 2 to get the average crown spread, or ACS.

Then the height is checked with a clinometer, a calibrated instrument that is quite accurate if read correctly. They will measure out from the highest branch 100 feet and then look through the clinometer, which gives a reading of the height from their eye to that highest point of the tree. Then they sight the bottom of the tree and add or subtract this measurement from the tree height, depending on whether the persons eye level is higher or lower than the base of the tree at 100 feet away. What you end up with is the vertical height, or VH. A GPS reading is then taken, and the tree is checked over to report the condition as excellent, good, fair, or poor.

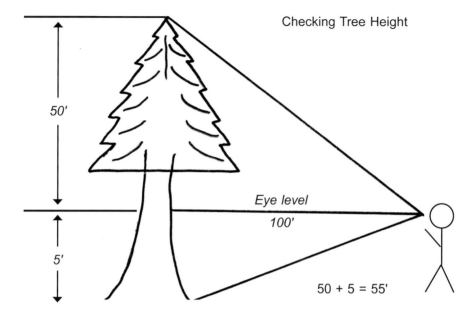

The tree is then scored with a point system and compared with others on the list. The total points are determined by adding the circumference in inches to the height in feet, and then adding one-quarter of the average crown spread in feet. So a tree with 75 inches CBH, 100 feet VH, and 60 feet ACS is scored as 75 + 100 + 15 = 190 total points.

Keep in mind that some types of tree do not grow very large. You may not be very impressed by a champion gray birch or an American chestnut unless you have some idea of what an average-size tree of the species looks like.

While you are out searching, be sure to look at the surrounding trees. If you come to a grove that consists of mostly one type of tree, be sure to look for the largest one. Then when you do see the champion of that type, you will appreciate it a bit more.

Check the New Hampshire Big Tree web site at http://extension. unh.edu/Trees/NH-Big-Tree-Program for updates on the trees listed in this book.

New Hampshire's National Champion Trees

New Hampshire has seven national champion trees. Two of them are shown in this book. The black spruce pictured on page 70 is a national champion, and is located in Jefferson, New Hampshire. You can see the national champion black spruce at Pondicherry park in tour number 20 (see page 103). The pitch pine pictured on page 114 is also a national champion, located in Newbury, New Hampshire.

Key to Measurement abbreviations

CBH: Circumference Breast height
VH: Vertical Height
ACS: Average Crown Spread

NOTE: All maps are oriented so that North is ↑.

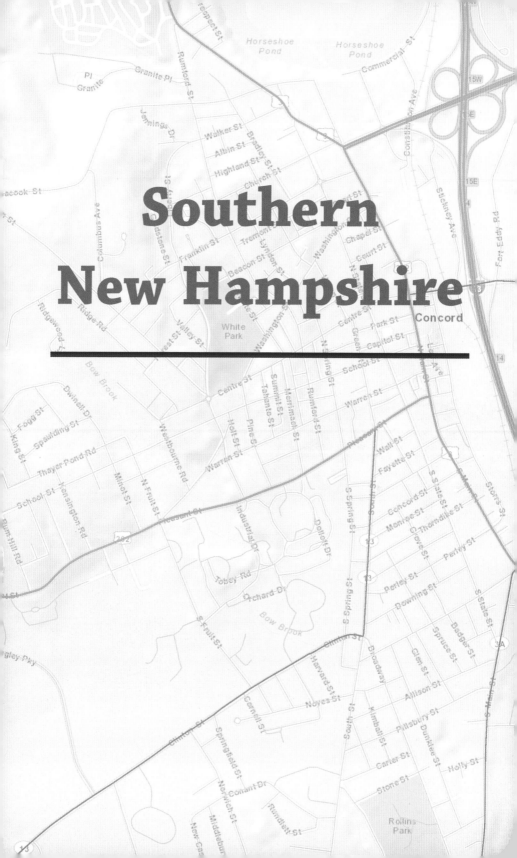

Southern
New Hampshire

Concord

Shagbark Hickory

Shagbark Hickory

Carya ovate

T his type of tree is easily identified by its shaggy bark, which curls away from the trunk, and by the medium-size nuts in a hard green shell. It is common in some areas of southern New Hampshire and grows with oaks and pines. There are many good-sized hickory trees in Strafford County, with the three largest in the county very close in size and in total Big Tree Program points.

This tall and wide-crowned example is in an open field on Adams Point in Durham. The lower branch, with a swing tied to it, is leaning to the ground, as though it is helping to hold the Ole Hickory up. It is growing near the former house site of Captain Edward Adams, the last builder, owner, and operator of a Piscataqua gundalow. His family lived here for generations and operated a turn-of-the-century boardinghouse for tourists. There is now a monument to some family members at their gravesite nearby.

I associate this hickory with turkeys because a small flock of them flew overhead into the woods while I was measuring the tree. Wildlife loves hickory nuts, so if you want to try these nuts (they are good), you should act quickly in the fall before the turkeys, squirrels, and deer get them.

I have used the lumber of this kind of tree for replacing many tool handles because it is a strong and longwearing wood. My cross-country skis have a hickory base. The wood was also once used for the rims and spokes of wagon wheels.

The land at Adams Point was donated to the state and is managed by New Hampshire Fish and Game. The waterfront on the bay is frequented by waterfowl hunters in the fall and winter, keeping alive the tradition that the Adamses held dear. The nearby Jackson Estuarine Laboratory conducts research and provides data for the sound management of this important estuary called Great Bay.

The Adams Point hickory provides a great shady oasis on a hot summer day.

Adams Point is an interesting place to walk, so you don't have to end your visit at the tree. A trail follows the edge of the bay along some small cliffs with nice water views and great sunsets. Bird-watchers will appreciate the variety of waterfowl and other birds that migrate through here.

Difficulty rating 1

124" CBH   93' VH   77' ACS   Total points 236   Excellent Condition
GPS: N 43° 05.514'   W 070° 52.026'

Directions

Take Durham Point Road off Route 108 either from the Durham or Newmarket end. About halfway, or just under 4 miles along the road, is a side road, Adams Point Road, with a gate that is open on the bay side of the road. Go all the way to the end, past the boat launch and up the hill, to a parking area for the walking trails, which take off in front of a kiosk. If the kiosk parking area is full, you can park at Jackson lab, just across the road.

The shagbark hickory is near the edge of the field. Take the short trail to the field from the lookout that is just behind the kiosk. At the field take another trail to the right and go about 250 feet to the tree.

White Ash
Fraxinus americana

This tall tree is growing in the woods on conservation land in Atkinson. White ash trees grow to a great size, and although this one is not the largest in the state, it is among the largest and is the tallest example. You will notice the five to nine (usually seven) leaflets growing on each stem and the cigar-shaped seedpods growing in clusters. The gray bark has a noticeable braided look that helps identify the tree.

The lumber of the ash is important for the sporting world with uses such as baseball bats, hockey sticks, and snowshoes. I have used the wood for oars, paddles, and for steam-bent stems and ribs for small boats. It is a light but strong wood that steam-bends easily, resists impacts, and is flexible.

The Sawyer conservation land was set aside by the town for use by the public. A forest management plan has been developed to enhance the different types of tree growth found on the parcel, and will provide wildlife with specific types of habitat for their benefit. This white ash was singled out in the plan as an exemplary ash worthy of preserving. The property has been recently logged, and the sale of the timber that is cut can provide funds that allow the town to continue managing the land. I associate this ash with osprey because one was calling from the top of the tree when I was trying to find it.

Difficulty rating 2

180" CBH 119' VH 87' ACS Total points 331 Excellent Condition
GPS: N 42° 49.381' W 071° 08.616'

Atkinson Ash

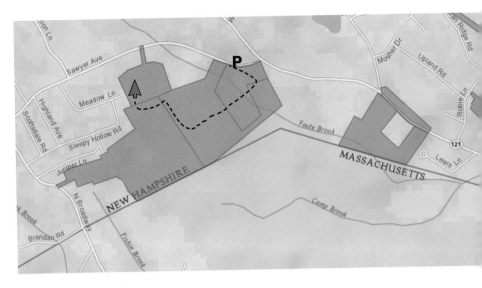

Map for Atkinson Ash

Directions

Take Route 121 from Route 125 in Haverhill, Massachusetts, or from Route 111 in Hampstead. From Haverhill take a left off Route 121 onto Sawyer Road. Park in the parking area for the Sawyer conservation land (on the left just as you turn onto Sawyer Road). Walk down the main trail and bear slightly left and then straight. The trail is marked with blue markers. Follow this main trail until you go over an intermittent stream with a few elms near it. Afterwards, keep an eye out for the red trail that crosses the blue trail. Go right on the red trail for a short distance and look for the yellow trail markers. Take the yellow trail. It may be hard to see because the recent logging has allowed more sunlight in to the forest floor and low brush and raspberries are growing in. Keep on the trail along a stonewall wall until it ends at markers where the blue trail starts again. Go through the break in the wall on the left following the blue trail and head toward the houses that are along the road. A few hundred feet beyond the stonewall you will see the white ash some distance off on the right. Go toward it and step over another stonewall to a lot near a house when you see the tree.

A Wild and Scenic River Big Tree Tour

This is a tour of trees that are on conserved land near the Lamprey River. This river has been declared a National Wild and Scenic River in the towns of Epping, Lee, Durham, and Newmarket. Through the natural resource studies that were completed in order to nominate the river to the national program, a few large trees were documented. Years later I searched them out, along with others already listed in the Big Tree Program, and measured them. The trees include red pine, northern white cedar, white pine, American chestnut, northern red oak, and swamp white oak. Most stops to see them take about fifteen minutes except for the red pine and American chestnut, which require a longer round-trip hike of three hours and one and a half hours, respectively. The whole tour would take most of a day, depending on how long you linger at each site. If less time is available, the two longer hikes could be planned for another day. However you plan it, take your time and enjoy this nationally recognized treasure.

Lamprey River Rocks

Northern White Cedar

Growing in the corner of the Central Cemetery, this white cedar was planted here and in many cemeteries because cedars are known as a symbol of eternity, and they add some greenery in the stark winters. They usually grow in swamps up north, but some are planted in southern New Hampshire as a landscape tree. Atlantic white cedar is found in the swamps of the southern part of the state. It looks as though this one has lost some of its top in a storm because it is not as symmetrical as it once was. This tree is near the center of Epping across the street from the former high school, Watson Academy.

Northern white cedar in Epping

Difficulty rating 1

90" CBH   59' VH   32' ACS   Total points 157   Good condition

GPS: N 43° 02.583'   W 071° 04.456'

Δ **County Champion**

American Chestnut

We have all heard of chestnuts roasting on an open fire, but hardly anyone roasts them anymore because they are not common. The Chestnut blight, which was imported into the country from Japan around 1900, has infected them and kills the trees off before they can reach the grand stature they once had. They were as common as the oaks are now, and the rot resistant lumber had many uses. Some of the canoes and rowboats that I have restored had chestnut stems and gunwales.

This tree is the largest recorded in the state, although its 44-inch circumference is not all that big. It does have some chestnuts in their prickly husks that may help spread new growth in the area. Maybe this is the tree that will spread blight resistant genes, so you should leave the nuts so the squirrels and birds can spread them around.

Difficulty rating 2 - Boots for stream crossings are suggested

41" CBH   82' VH   32' ACS   Total points 131   Good condition

GPS: N 43° 03.203'   W 071° 01.610'

Δ State Champion

Eastern White Pine

This eastern white pine is one of the largest you will see along the Lamprey River. The county champion pine that is a half-mile away on private land has two or three trunks joined together to make one tree. That one may be bigger, but this tree is more impressive. The national Big Tree Program is now discussing whether to make separate categories for single- and multiple-stemmed trees. The single-stemmed tree highlighted here is in the George Falls Woods, which is owned by the town of Epping and managed as a pine forest. The trail brings you in a loop with a spur down to the pine and the Lamprey River.

Difficulty rating 1

127" CBH   100' VH   61' ACS   Total points 242   Excellent condition

GPS: N 43° 03.214'   W 071° 01.360'

Riverside Farm Oak

This red oak is not listed with the Big Tree Program because there are many larger oaks in the county and state. But it is such a special tree that I could not pass up including it as part of this tour. It is not small by any means, and it is one of few that you will find of this size in a woodland setting. This is a healthy tree that is straight and tall. The Homeowners Association of Riverside Farm Drive owns the property. When the farm property was developed, an agreement was worked out where part of the land was developed for homes, and a working farm was left on about forty acres. The rest of the acreage was set aside as common land for the homeowners to enjoy. This is not public property, so please respect the owners and go to view just the tree and do not wander around on the rest of the land.

It takes 4 kids to reach around this red oak.

Difficulty rating 1

150" CBH   94' VH   70' ACS   Total points 257   Excellent condition

GPS: N 43° 05.513'   W 071° 01.280'

Swamp White Oak

Growing near the edge of Tuttle Swamp in Newmarket, this swamp white oak is the current county champion. It is a good-sized tree and you can see different forest stages on the way out to it. The first part of the trail has been clear-cut at one point and the young shrubs and small trees are filling out the land. This type of cover is important for many small mammals and birds. You will notice the difference in forest types at the old boundary line where this oak is located. The former county champion was a much larger swamp white oak that fell before this book went to print. If you go across the woods to the north toward the power lines you can see the stump and fallen tree in the high grass and shrubs. You should also be able to notice how hollow the old tree was and can see the space it required in the woods there.

This swamp white oak forest is in one of a few small pockets along the Lamprey River where you will find this species. It is like a separate forest in itself. The trees grow at the edge of the swamp, where it is too wet for most other trees; and it survives the annual overflow of the wetlands here in the spring and during heavy rains. These areas are important for the wood ducks, which land in the deeper water nearby in the fall and then swim into the flooded forest to feed on the acorns.

Difficulty rating 1   Could be wet in the spring, wear boots and spray for protection from ticks.

114" CBH   68' VH   52' ACS   Total Points 234   Good Condition
GPS: N 43° 04.823'   W 070° 59.631
Δ County Champion
165" CBH   72' VH   79' ACS   Total points 278   Fallen-Dead
GPS: N 43° 04.858'   W 070° 59.703'
Δ Former county champion

Wood ducks will feed on the acorns in the swamp white oak woods.

Directions

Start the Lamprey River Tour in Epping at the white cedar, in the Central Cemetery on the corner of Main Street and Prescott Road. Park in front of the cemetery off Main Street; the tree is in the back corner by the house. After viewing this cedar, return to your car and head north up Main Street, bear right at the fork onto North River Road, and then right again onto Old Hedding Road. Go to and then cross Route 125 at the lights and continue on Old Hedding Road to its end. Turn right onto Route 87 (Hedding Road) and go about ¼ mile to a dirt road on the left; it is closed to vehicle traffic just before the Amethyst House and the river.

Pull in and park in front of the stones in the small parking area. Walk down the dirt road about half a mile. You will have to cross Rum Brook, which has washed out the road, so be careful during high water.

After the brook, go a little way up the hill and then go right into the gated gravel pit. Walk all the way to the other end, where the trail exits the gravel pit. Then bear right on the trail through the boulders. Go left at the fork; it will bring you down near the river. The chestnut tree is on the right just before you get to a swampy area.

To continue the tour to the eastern white pine, return to your car and keep going down Route 87. Take the first left after the river onto Jacobs Well Road. Go past Windsor Lane on the left and keep a lookout for a fence gate at the George Falls Woods, on the left. You can park off the road at the gate or at any pull-off nearby.

Walk past the gate and follow the trail down toward the river. The pine is on the trail just before the river. This property consists of a very good pine forest that is managed by the Epping Conservation Commission.

To find the next tree on the tour, head back along the trail to your car. Then continue driving down Jacobs Well Road and go left onto Camp Lee Road. Follow it to the end at Wadleigh Falls, and then take a left to cross the river. Follow Route 152 along the river and then around the corner. Just after Kustra's Auto Body, you can park on the right before the snowmobile trail that crosses the road.

Walk across the street and follow the trail beside Kustra's about half a mile to the red oak. When ready go back on Route 152 toward Newmarket. About a mile down the road, look for a guardrail at a corner in the road. Just after that is a pullover on the right and parking for a few cars at the Tuttle Swamp Conservation Area.

Follow the path in front of you a few hundred feet and then go right onto another trail that cuts across in the tall grass. Follow that trail a hundred feet or so to the edge of the taller woods. Follow the boundary to the left that separates the 2 stages of forests. The tree is a few hundred feet down on the boundary line. From here you can see the clearing off behind you for the power lines where the other fallen oak is located.

This is a good place to end the Lamprey River tour, but be sure to wander a little in the swamp white oak forest around you before heading back to your car.

Red Pine

Pinus resinosa

T his type of pine is also known as Norway pine even though it is native to the eastern United States. Many are planted throughout the state of New Hampshire because they are known as fast-growing trees. They will grow in quickly after a fire and love the sandy soils we have here near the river.

This tree, on the boundary that separated the two properties that are now combined to make up the Lamprey River Forest, is the second largest in circumference for its type in the state. It has a long, clear trunk and must have been here quite a bit longer than other nearby trees of the same type. There is a grove of planted trees on the property that is worth a visit to see as an example of a healthy middle-aged red pine forest. To appreciate the size of this red pine, be sure to see the grove first (it is just a little farther up the trail) and then go back to visit the Big Tree.

The Lamprey River Forest is part of an early local conservation effort that included the town of Epping, private donations, the Society for the Protection of New Hampshire Forests (SPNHF), and the Lamprey River Wild and Scenic Program. The aim was to protect the health of the river by conserving land along it. The neighboring land was added later to conserve a long stretch of the Lamprey in West Epping that is owned and managed by the Society for the Protection of New Hampshire Forests (SPNHF).

Difficulty rating 3 Some off trail travel. GPS needed.

91" CBH   96' VH   37' ACS   Total Points 196   Fair Condition
GPS: N 43° 02.615'   W 071° 07.148'
Δ County Champion

Red Pine

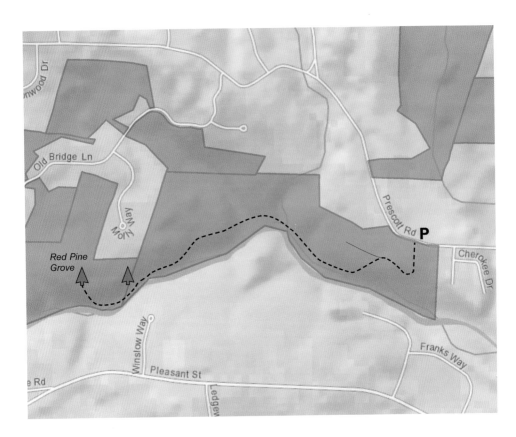

Directions

Get off Route 101 at the Depot Road exit in West Epping. Follow Depot Road and cross Route 27 onto Blake Road. Go 1.3 miles and take a right onto Prescott Road. Go 1.7 miles to a sign for Lamprey River Forest on the right. Pull in and park, leaving room for farm vehicles to get in and out of the nearby fields.

Follow the edge of the back field on the left and you will come to the trail. A half-mile or so in, take care to stay near a stream after you cross it as the trail is hard to locate there. Follow the trail to the river. Follow the river upstream. The trail dies out and the land rises, so you will have to walk through the woods and keep the river within sight. If you keep the river to your left, you will come back to a level trail. As you get close to the GPS coordinates, keep going a few hundred feet farther along the river until you see the grove of red pines on the right. Then come back to the Big Tree.

Black Tupelo
Nyssa sylvatica

T he state champion tupelo is very impressive for its type and is significant because it is considerably larger than others in the state. Also called black gum, these trees look prehistoric with their chunky bark and branches that start out horizontal but then turn like an elbow and grow straight up to the sky. Not being very desirable for lumber or firewood was a saving grace in allowing them to grow to an old age. Some in New Hampshire are more than 500 years old and have been noted as the oldest trees in New England. I am not sure of the age of these particular trees, but it may have been over 400 years since they sprouted up from the swamp.

The lumber has been used at times for things such as soles of shoes and hubs of wheels because it is longer wearing than other woods. Yes, shoe soles were named for these trees, not for a gummy or sappy mixture that is often thought of when you hear of gum soles. A honey is made from the flowers of the tupelo that is so good that Van Morrison sang a popular song about his girl being as sweet as "Tupelo Honey."

This hike includes three trees in the same woods to show the life stages. There are also smaller gum trees around that are good examples of the type and are in excellent condition. The large one you should see first is a dead tree that fell over. I found it when it was still standing and there was a neat rounded doorway in the bottom of the trunk that reminded me of the home of Winnie the Pooh or other storybook figures. With the trunk now on its side you can clearly see how hollow some of these trees can get. The next example is still living, but the bark looks different from the healthy gum trees and is starting to come off in areas. It may have been hit by lightning and is on its way out. This one has the third largest circumference of any tupelo in the state, so is very large and shows the way the hummocks are formed under the tree providing a place for new growth to root when the giant falls to the wet swamp.

This large gum is showing its age.

Then finally you come to the king of New Hampshire gum trees. This is a real beauty, and is impressive to stand in front of in its natural environment. The bark is chunky and looks prehistoric, clearly an impressive tree. I hope it retains the state champ status for some time.

The property these trees are on is called the Mast Road Natural Area, owned and managed by the Southeast Land Trust of New Hampshire. This group has helped conserve many properties in the area by holding conservation easements and accepting outright ownership of some lands. The organization commits much time and energy to managing the lands for the betterment of the communities they are in. This parcel connects with other nearby conserved properties and provides a large block of undeveloped land, which is necessary for some kinds of wildlife to continue to thrive in this heavily populated part of the state. This parcel also connects to the Lamprey River, on which I live and enjoy so much.

The land is quite flat and wet, so be prepared to wear boots or, better yet, make this a winter snowshoe trip. Some dirt trails have been rutted up and filled with water, so you will need to go around these areas into the brushy side paths. Sometimes it is even easier to go off the trails into the woods while walking. Some new trails have been made to bypass the wet tote roads and recent improvements to the property should make the traveling easier. You will definitely need your GPS to find the trees here and to get back out.

Difficulty rating 3 to 4

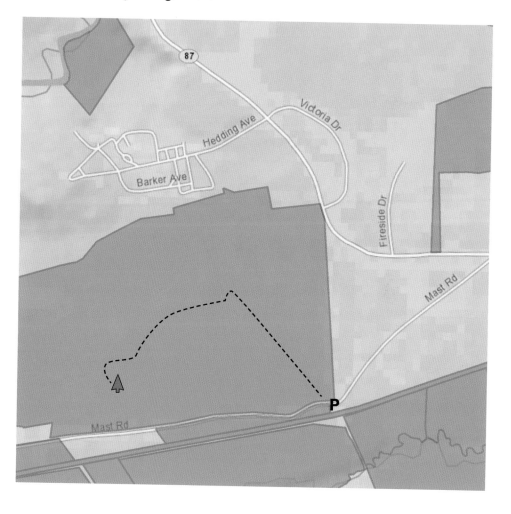

View the trees in this order for the best effect. Trails grown over and wet but flat, bushwhacking required:

Dead Tree:
Dead, no measurements. Fell over in 2013.
GPS: N 43° 02.162'   W 071° 01.713'

Dying Tree:
105" CBH   61' VH   38' ACS   176 Total Points   Poor Condition
GPS: N 43° 02.199'   W 071° 01.759'

Biggest Tree:
132" CBH   89' VH   58' ACS   236 Total Points   Good Condition
GPS: N 43° 02.126'   W 071° 01.695'
Δ State Champion

Directions

To get there, take Route 125 in Epping to Route 87, also known as Hedding Road. About 2 miles down look for a sharp right onto Mast Road. Go down about a mile to a pullover on the left and park there. It is a walk of about 1½ miles from here, and you should see some wildlife on the way. It is best to cross the street and go straight through an orange gate onto the tote road.

This is the newly improved main north trail. After about ½ mile it ends close to Hedding Campground. Take the main west trail toward the trees and go another ¾ mile. In dry years you should be able to get near the trees by taking the trail most of the way. In wet years, when you get to an area where it seems very wet all around you, just go into the woods on the left and head toward the trees. You will start seeing some nice healthy tupelos and quite a few small sassafras trees, which are significant in quantity for southern New Hampshire. Eventually you'll come to the first tupelo tree. The others are all within a few hundred feet from it.

When ready to leave, if you have had enough bushwhacking, you could find your way out to the road by listening for the few cars driving by, take a compass reading, and walk to the road and back to your vehicle. Recent improvements to the property may allow access close to the tree along Mast Road for those who want a shorter walk.

Eastern Hophornbeam
Ostrya virginiana

This is a native tree of the eastern United States that should not be confused with the American hornbeam. The hophornbeam is called ironwood because its sawn lumber is very tough, strong, and hard, while the hornbeam is called musclewood because its smooth bark with ridges and waves resembles muscles. The Eastern hophornbeam is a medium-sized tree with fruits that ripen in September in cone-like clusters that resemble hops. The strong wood has been used for wedges for felling trees and for gears in the old mills. Some native tribes took wood at the heart of the branches, cut it into bits, and boiled them, making a decoction to drink that was said to help with kidney troubles.

State champion Eastern hophornbeam

This example is located on Brackett Road, in Rye, at the edge of the salt marshes on land that is now owned by the town and managed by the Rye Conservation Commission. The tree is not very big but is significant in New Hampshire for its type. If you look around a little and go past the ledges to the other side toward the salt marsh, you will see a number of small hophornbeams along with some larger ones. Look for a forked tree in particular that has one fork almost as big as this state co-champion. It is two trees joined together that could almost be counted as one, which would make it a national champion.

The history at this site is interesting as it is called Remick's Island after the family that has lived in the area since the colonial days. The story goes that in 1691 a group of Indians from what is now York, Maine, swooped down on the farmers in the area and killed more than twenty people, burned their homes, and captured some of the women and children. One of the captured Brackett children returned years

later as an adult and reclaimed her land here. You can see the grave-stones from the massacre at the Brackett Burial Grounds, just across the stream from this site.

Difficulty rating 2

78" CBH   82' VH   42' ACS   Total Points 141   Good Condition

GPS: N 43° 00.976'   W 070° 44.536'

Δ State Co-Champion

Directions

To get to this tree, take Brackett Road from Washington Road in Rye, go just under a half-mile, and look for a white historical marker and a pullover on the right after a stream that goes into the salt marsh. You can park here and take a look at the burial grounds in the small woods there. Then walk down the road over the stream and look on the left for a trail just past a large stone. It is hard to see, so don't pass it by. Follow that trail in about a half mile and you will come to a point where it becomes hard to follow and you will see a rock ledge or a small cliff in front of you with a bit of water at the bottom (in most years). This state champion tree is near the trail about 150 feet back from the ledge toward where you came in.

Big Trees Benefit Wildlife

As you look at these large trees, keep an eye out for signs of use by the wild creatures in the area. The older trees have been there through generations of birds, animals, and humans. I have noticed wildlife at most of the sites either very near the trees or in them. I like to say that a partridge led me to a large black gum (tupelo) that I was searching for during partridge hunting season. I looked for the tree I had heard about in the area a few times with no luck. One day a partridge flew up off a trail into the thick brush, I circled a few times looking for it and came upon the tree. I never did find the partridge. It was in the same woods where I was searching for a black gum tree that I had seen earlier but for which I had not taken a GPS reading. I was hot and sweaty after wandering for some time, getting turned around because the woods all looked the same. I was almost ready to give up when a rabbit went bounding into a swampy area and I went toward it, looked up, and lo and behold what turned out to be the state champion black gum tree was right there.

Many of the Big Trees get heart rot in the center, which creates a cavity that provides a nesting area and shelter for rabbits, porcupines, raccoons, and some types of birds. In very large trees, even bears can use the hollow trunks to hibernate. The tall trees also are ideal roosting sites for large birds of prey. You may see or hear hawks, owls, and eagles using the high perches to scout out the area.

The fruit, nuts, and cones of the Big Trees can produce large crops that are a boon to the wildlife in the area. They may feed there in the morning or late afternoon, so if you time your visit and keep quiet, you may get a glimpse of some of the birds or animals that come to the tree. Not too long ago local people would also note when the trees produced bumper crops of berries or nuts, then collect the bounty to help get them through the long New Hampshire winter.

Storybook setting at the base of a large dead gum tree.

Nashua Big Tree Tour

The city of Nashua, New Hampshire—near the New Hampshire-Massachusetts border—is known as the Gate City because of its proximity to Boston. Money magazine has twice cited Nashua as "the best place to live in America." The Nashua River meets the Merrimac River here as it flows through the city toward the ocean.

When first settled, this area was under constant attack by the local Penacook tribes, who were loathe to give up their important hunting and fishing grounds. After a 1724 battle in which seven settlers were killed, an Abenaki warrior carved an Indian head in a tree on the north bank of the Nashua River. The settlers named the land there Indian Head. Years later the Middlesex Canal was built to connect the Merrimac River to Boston. This opened up trade to the world. After a canal boat named Nashua was built with much fanfare, Indian Head Village was renamed Nashua. It went on to become an important manufacturing center and today is thriving with new commercial industries.

There are several nice parks and some older sections of the city where you will find the larger trees. Start the tour by entering into town off Route 101A/Amherst Street and take a left onto Sargeant Avenue. Then park either at the tennis courts off Artillery Lane on the right, or go up to the North Common ball fields at the next right on Greeley lane, and park there.

Don your walking shoes or get on your bike and head out to your first stop at the Edgewood Cemetery, off Route 10. You enter it off Cushing Avenue by going back on Sergeant Avenue to Dartmouth on the right then left on Cushing to the cemetery. Walk or ride through the sugar maples to some big pines in the back. In the fall the many sugar maples spread their branches over the roadways and gravestones. Their bright yellow leaves make a very calming and peaceful scene. Work your way to the northern end to see an interesting stone chapel that is close to where the biggest pines are. While not big enough to merit measurement, some of the pines are over 10 feet in circumference and have the thick bark that the large trees show.

Chapel at the Edgewood Cemetery

This is a worthwhile place to start your visit in town. The cemeteries provide some of the best scenery in the cities, with their many planted ornamental trees, impressive gravestones, and some nice buildings to boot. Just be sure to respect the graves (you don't want to disturb the spirits) and try sticking to the roadways or paths for the most part. When your time is up (Ha), leave the way you came in and then go over to Artillery Lane, pass the front of Holman Stadium, and go around toward the town ball fields at the rear of the stadium. You can see a few large silver maples here on private property, so just look from the road. You will get a chance to see one up close soon.

Continue to where Greeley Street goes off on the right and follow it across Merrimac Street to Abbott Street. Go right on Abbott to the Speare Museum and into the parking area behind the building. Right in the parking lot you will see the second-largest black walnut in the state at 157 inches around. If you are there in the fall, there will likely be walnut husks on the ground. These are very tough to open but worth the effort to get out the nice nuts inside. The tree itself is big and healthy looking with a wide spreading crown and good height. I have used black walnut to make small jewelry boxes, and it is known as an excellent wood for furniture and other wooden items. It has a rich dark color that most other woods cannot compare to and commands a premium price at the lumberyards. After some time checking out the tree, you may want to tour the museum and take in some of the culture this city has to offer. The Florence A. Speare Museum was built in the early 1970s to showcase the history of Nashua. It houses changing exhibits and a research library and is open Tuesdays and Thursdays. Right next door is the Federal Revival style Abbott-Spaulding House, which was the home of some of the most prominent and influential families of Nashua.

The Abbott-Spaulding house with big trees in the side yard.

Come out of the parking area and turn right on Abbott. Take a left on French Street and then right on Merrimac to its end. The bur oak is on the left near the intersection with brick crosswalks. This is the only one listed in NH of its type. It is more common in the Midwestern part of the country. The main feature is its acorns with the caps almost covering the whole acorn.

Moss can also grow on these caps giving this tree its alternate name of mossy cup oak. Just look at this tree from the sidewalk. Then continue by crossing the street onto Mt Pleasant Street past the school and go all the way to its end on Concord Street

Cross at a safe spot and go north on Concord to a tuliptree a short way up on the right. These trees are noticeable in many cities for their large size and tall, straight trunks. They are common in the southern states and are grown here only as ornamentals. If you visit in the spring, look for their tulip-

The bur oak has unusual acorns.

photo by Anne Krantz

like flowers. This specimen is on private property, so respect the home-owner and just look from the sidewalk.

Continue on to a right turn onto Swart Street and then go to the Swart Terrace Circle at the end. There is a larch at the start of the circle that may be a hybrid. At first I thought it was European, and it has a larger circumference than any European larch in the state. It would be co-champion with another at the state nursery in Boscawen that is much taller. These were planted in many towns because they grew better in urban settings than the native larches. My last visit to the tree left me thinking it was not European and probably not the Japanese version that I have also seen in Boscawen. Hybrids of the two were known to be planted and this may be one of them.

The larches and the rare dawn redwood are some of the few conifers that shed their needles for the winter. If the needles are on, the larch is a very nice looking tree as it turns a golden color in the fall. Otherwise it is quite stark and barren looking in the winter.

From here go back to Concord Street, go right a short distance to Greeley park and take a lunch break. There is a playground wading pool and several labeled trees on both sides of the road, including one named eastern larch behind the stone building. It has a more golden top in the fall and a different type of cone than the tree on Swart Terrace. Head back on Concord the way you came and then go to the second left on East Stark Street and go to the end. Go right on Atherton and follow it until you come to Atherton Park, with its basketball courts and grassy lawn. Along the edge of the roads is a line of large, wide-crowned silver maples. The biggest one, at 201 inches circumference, is impressive with its twisted trunk and hollow center that draws you in to look. These maples are water lovers and grow along many rivers in the area. This bunch is quite close to the Merrimac River. Be sure to look over the deeply furrowed sharp leaves with a noticeable silver color on the underside.

Silver maple in Atherton Park

Continue on past Atherton Park to the end of the road then go right on Lock Road. You can follow that all the way up to Concord Road and then go back to where you started. The total distance is 5.5 miles. This is fine if biking but if you are walking and want to make the tour shorter you could start at Greeley park and make a round trip to see most of the trees. Then drive over to the cemetery. This shortens the walk to a more manageable 3.5 miles

The Mine Falls Park, on the other side of town, is well known for its trails along the river. So if you want to spend more time walking or biking, you could go there or check out the downtown area.

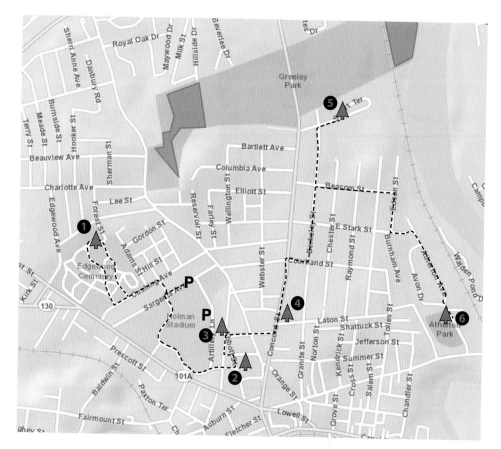

Difficulty rating 2 Watch for traffic.

1. Edgewood Cemetery Pines

124" CBH

2. Black Walnut

157" CBH   86' VH   88' ACS   Total Points 265 Good Condition
GPS: N 42° 45.990'   W 071° 28.093'
Δ County Champion

3. Bur Oak

84" CBH   67' VH   50' ACS   Total Points 164 Excellent Condition
GPS: N 42° 46.115'   W 071° 28.195'
Δ State Champion

4. Tuliptree

131" CBH   84' VH   59' ACS   Total Points 230   Good Condition

GPS: N 42°46.228'   W 071° 27.698'

5. Larch

118" CBH   79' VH   56' ACS   Total Points 212   Fair Condition

GPS: N42° 46.716'   W 071° 27.767'

6. Silver Maple

201" CBH   82' VH   74' ACS   Total Points 302   Fair Condition

GPS: N 42° 46.168'   W 071° 27.322'

Mockernut Hickory
Carya tomentosa

Viewing this species of hickory requires a short uphill walk of maybe ten minutes through some farm fields. The tree is in the middle of the second field up, so you cannot miss it. The first thing you will notice is that the trunk is quite hollow. It seems as if it is standing on four legs with the hollow showing on all sides and the trunk wood is holding on just at the outer edges. It makes you wonder how much longer it will hold up under some of the strong winds that must blow on the hillside. There is enough wood to allow the ground-water to rise up the tree and feed the many leaves that still show. The leaf scars are what help tell the difference between this species and the closely related pignut hickory. The more common shagbark hickory has its noticeable shaggy bark, which makes it easier to identify.

Mockernut hickory on four legs

The land on which this tree grows is part of the Bragdon Farm and is open to the public for conservation and recreational uses. The Amherst Junior Women's Club supplied materials for the benches at the top part of the field, and the Conservation Commission in the town put them together. The benches overlook the tree and the farm, and aside from busy Route 101 it makes for a nice place to relax.

If you walk farther up the hill, you will go past some pitch pines into another open area at the top of the hill. From 1936 to the early 1970s, the hill was used as a local ski area with a ski tow up to the top and a ticket booth down near the highway. The former cow path under the highway has been improved to allow walking to the other side, where the hill is still used for tobogganing.

Difficulty rating 2

122" CBH   95' VH   48' ACS   Total points 229   Fair Condition

GPS: N 42° 54.319'   W 071° 34.519'

Δ State Champion

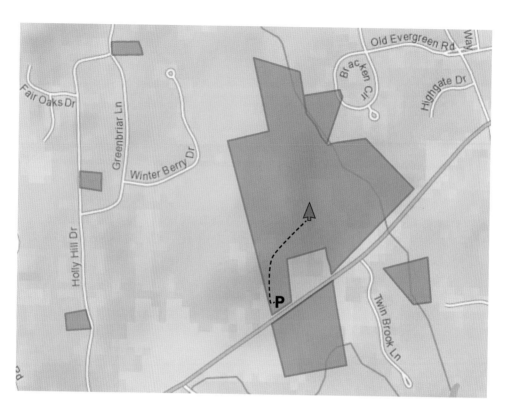

Directions

This tree is located off Route 101 in Amherst near the Bedford town line. There are signs on the highway marking the entrance to the parking area. This is a busy road, so be careful pulling in and out. Park and then follow the tote road to the left and go up the hill above where you parked. To see the hickory, go through the opening in the stonewall with red cedar trees standing guard and into the second field up.

Atlantic White Cedar
Chamaecyparis thyoides

T his species is at the northern end of its range in New Hampshire growing only in the southern part of the state. There are pure stands in some wet areas scattered here and there in this part of the state. These 89 acres of land were donated to the Society for the Protection of New Hampshire Forests (SPNHF) in 1972 to manage for its wildlife and natural features. SPNHF is one of the oldest conservation organizations in the country and has been helping to protect New Hampshire forests for over a hundred years.

This unique area around Powwow River and the nearby ponds constitutes a large part of the state's Atlantic white cedar woods. Much of it is held in conservation for future generations to enjoy. The Webster Wildlife and Natural Area in Kingston is a perfect place to view these trees and see how they grow along the edges of the river and ponds and in the low, wet areas in between. You can also get a wonderful view of these woods from a distance by paddling down the slow-moving Powwow River from an access off New Boston Road.

Quite a few years back my brother and I hauled some of this light cedar wood out of the swamps at Wash Pond in Hampstead, New Hampshire. We were able to carry most of the 8- to 12-foot large-diameter logs out on our shoulders to where we could get at them with a truck. The lumber is a fair alternative for northern white cedar, but it can get harder and will curl or warp more often when sawn for boat planking.

Start out the hike at the farthest trail to get a good walk in and see most of the area. At first you will see many pines and hemlocks with a few large ones on the side of the trail. There are also some small black spruces scattered in this area, which is not too common in this part of the state. Keep an eye out for red pine, and you may see some pitch pine farther up the trail too. As you go along there will be a few signs on the right marking private property, so stay out on the main trail. After the

The pleasing bark of the Atlantic white cedar

private areas, there are some side trails off to the right that will bring you to a bench near the river. Then small trails go along the river edge ending at a large area of pure cedars. If you want to get an idea what a true dense cedar swamp is like, look through these woods and try to pick out the large cedars. This is a workout—jumping from tree to tree, pushing aside the thick brush, and all the while trying not to step in the deeper water in between. When trying to pick out the big cedars in this dense growth, the one you are working hard to get to ends up just looking big because the one behind it has blended right in, making two trees look like one. I did not find the biggest trees in there, but who is to say that you won't? Keep working your way around the edges of the cedars until you come back to the main trail.

If you do not want to wander too much, then you can avoid following the river and looking through the swamps by staying on the main trail instead of taking that right turn toward the river. After some time you will see Cedar Swamp Pond on the left through the trees with some tall pines but mostly cedars all around the edge of it. Cedar

#1 is near the pond and is tall at 75 feet but has a smaller circumference at 61 inches. Cedar #2 is in the same general area; we should call it Mister Twister because of the twisted look of its bark. I am sure the wood under it has the same twisted grain. This is the state's largest with 151 total points. It is an unusual looking tree that has great character and deserves the honor.

Mister Twister

Get back to the main trail and continue until you see cedar #3, which has the largest circumference. It is not mixed with nearby cedars and gives you a better view of the tree without too many others around it. That fact may prevent the tree from gaining another ten feet or so in height to be a clear champion over the other two shown. It will likely spread out some and continue growing in circumference because there are no trees nearby forcing it to grow taller to beat out its neighbors to the sunlight.

I measured about five trees while here and all had an average crown spread of about 20 feet and the total points were within 11 points. This seems to be about the maximum growth for Atlantic cedars in this part of New Hampshire. I know they get bigger in the warmer climates down south. I did not check all the cedar woods in this spot, so this may offer you a good chance to find a champion tree and nominate it yourself. Let's associate these trees with the white-tailed deer as I have seen their tracks all around. They like to browse on the leaves while the heavy cover the trees provide keeps the snow depth down in the winter. I noticed rabbit tracks too, and in the heaviest part of the cedar swamp some chickadees came around to greet me. They add some cheer to a winter hike. By the way I would encourage doing this trip in the winter. The frozen ground provides better walking for you in the swamps, and the trees will not suffer root damage as easily. The spring may be too wet.

Difficulty rating 3 You may need boots because of the wet areas; it could be rated a 4 if you want to tromp around in the heavy swamps to look for other trees.

1. Tallest White Cedar

61" CBH   75' VH   16' ACS   Total Points 140   Excellent Condition
GPS: N 42° 54.043'   W 071° 03.569'

2. "Mister Twister" White Cedar

73" CBH   73' VH   20' ACS   Total Points 151   Good Condition
GPS: N 42° 54.042'   W 071° 03.692'
Δ State Champion

3. Biggest Circumference White Cedar

78" CBH   66' VH   20' ACS   Total Points 149   Good Condition

GPS: N 42° 54.120'   W 071° 03.732'

Directions

To get to the Webster Natural Area, take Route 125 to Foley Brook Road in Kingston. Take an immediate right onto Frontage Road toward the fairgrounds and a dog park. Go left on Green Street. Pass the dog park and continue past the first parking area through a low spot with cedars. Park on the left in another parking area just before the road ends where you will see private drive signs. The main trails are easy to follow, and the three trees are not too far off them. You may need boots to get near the trees.

Captions for images on the following four pages:

1. *Ash along the Lamprey River*
2. *Black walnut in Nashua*
3. *Valley Cemetery black birch in Manchester*
4. *River birch in Swazey Parkway, Exeter*

Portsmouth Big Tree Tour

I am a native of Portsmouth and love this city and am sure you will too. It has a long history as a seaport and some of the trees have been around since the American Revolution. There are quite a few European beech trees spread throughout that grow to a great girth and were planted as ornamentals in front of the architecturally interesting buildings here.

This tour will take you to some of these historically significant homes, to a quiet park by the millpond, near the town offices, and to the South Cemetery. This is a good city for bike riding, so you can bring your bikes or take the time for a leisurely walk to absorb much that the city has to offer. There is so much to do here that you will likely have to come back a few times to get the feel of things. There are many top-notch restaurants and simpler sandwich shops when you get hungry. A rest stop can be made at Prescott Park, overlooking the Portsmouth Naval Shipyard on the mighty Piscataqua River. I have spent many a day here eating a Moe's Italian sandwich and enjoying the scenery. The historic homes offer tours, which can be fascinating if you want to know about the people who lived there and their connection to New Hampshire and our country.

You can take a ride on the new gundalow *Piscataqua*, which is a replica of the old sailing barges that were used to transport goods up and down the river. There is also a tour boat called the *Thomas Leighton* that will bring you seven miles out to sea to the Isles of Shoals. That should keep you busy, but let's get back to the trees.

To start your visit, you can leave your car at the parking area near the corner of Pleasant Street and Junkins Avenue or, if it's too full, try the parking garage in the center of the city off Hanover Street. Make your way to the Langdon House at 143 Pleasant Street to get started viewing the trees. The white house with a white fence has a European beech in the yard next to the house. At 192 inches in circumference you will get a feel of how big this type of tree can grow even though it is the smallest European beech that you will see on this tour. The grounds are open to the public, and you should be able to walk through the gate by the driveway. If not, ask to see the tree at the small building that sponsors the tours, if you allow enough time you may also consider paying the fee and take a tour of the main house. While visiting the grounds, be sure to go out back through the arbor to the softwood plantings. The state co-champion Douglas fir is there along with some impressive Norway spruce.

Go on toward downtown and up past the North Church. Keep going straight onto Market Street. Or, because this is a one-way road, if you're on a bike you will have to go right on State Street back just past the Langdon House and around to Bow Street, then to Market Street. You will enjoy the trip either way.

Moffatt-Ladd House and horse chestnut tree planted in 1776

Once on Market Street, go down a few blocks and you will see the Moffatt-Ladd House and its horse chestnut tree beside it. This is the largest of this type in the state, and it is no wonder due to its history. General William Whipple planted this tree in 1776 to celebrate his signing of the Declaration of independence and it is on the National Register of Historic Trees. One day I watched an arborist show his climbing skills and how he set up the cables that help keep the large limbs from breaking off. You can see the tree from the sidewalk or take a tour of the house and view it up close. Afterward, you could take a side trip through the garden area across the street into Ceres Street, with its restaurants and storefronts, then view the tugboats that work on the river and dock here.

Make your way back into the center of the city and go down Congress Street to the intersection with Middle Street. Take the crosswalk to the Discovery Center. You could visit there to learn more about the city and see some of the local art on exhibit. On the Islington Street side of the Discovery Center, take a look at the European linden in the side yard. This tree is similar to our native basswood but with smaller leaves. Both types are known for their soft lumber, which is sought after by wood-carvers because it is easy to work and will not crack or check.

European Beech

Continue back onto Middle Street, across State Street and then onto Route 1. You can take a side trip at the second right to Austin Street. Go two houses down and take a look from the sidewalk at the European beech inside the fence. There is another at the far end of the yard. These are big, but you can go on, not much farther, to see the second-largest one in the state.

Go down Route 1 to a left at the lights on Miller Avenue, also known as Route 1A. The Masonic Temple parking area is inside a fence on the left near the intersection. It is usually open, and you can go in and take a look at the European beech.

Continue on to the intersection with Rockland Street to see a Siberian elm, then go left on Rockland and right on Richards Avenue to get away from the busier Route 1A traffic. Go to the end and cross South Street to the South Cemetery. In the cemetery you will find a European larch on the South Street end. These trees were planted in the northeastern part of the United States and Canada and have become naturalized in the United States. This means they are recognized by American Forests as a tree that can reproduce naturally in areas where they are planted, and they are treated the same as a native tree in the Big Tree Program. This species is similar to our native tamarack, but the cones are a bit larger on the European version. The European larch canker has been spreading in some areas and can affect some native species like the tamarack. This specimen has some discoloration on the side, probably from a wound up higher on the side that caused the sap to drip down the tree. There are a few other European larches in the cemetery that are worth seeing in their fall colors, but this one has the second largest circumference of any tree of its type in the state.

Larch flowers

The larch is one of the few softwoods that has needles that turn golden yellow, then fall off for the winter. Some homes have them planted in the yard as ornamentals. Then the home sells in winter and the new owner cuts down the tree thinking that it has died because the needles have fallen off. In the southern part of the state, if you see these trees in November their golden needles will be at their best.

For those looking to add another tree to their identification skills, continue down a slight hill and then back up it to a green ash, which is at the side of the road near a small cedar grove. Green ash trees are not as large as the white ash, but don't pass this one by.

Be sure to check out some of the Norway spruces at the far end of the cemetery near Route 1A. Then walk or ride back to South Street and turn right into Clough Park. Just next door and inside the fence, you will see a crack willow. It does not have the familiar drooping branches of the weeping willow we all know, but it is closely related. Even though this tree is good sized and the county champion, crack willows can get quite a bit larger. Continue down the road to a left at Junkins Avenue and you will see the parking lot for the city offices on the right. This was the old hospital, and in between the parking lots is a large catalpa that is worth checking out. Catalpa trees have large leaves and long seedpods that hang off the branches all year long. I was not familiar with this tree, as I do not see them in the woods near where I live, but I remember seeing the seedpods on the sidewalks as a child living in town.

Head down Junkins Ave. past the millponds, and take a right on a small side road into Haven Park, near the start of this tour. This is a small park with green grass growing under a full canopy of good-sized oaks. The biggest is up near Pleasant Street across from the brick house. They must provide plenty of acorns to feed the huge gray squirrels that live here. You will also see an American beech down near the South Mill Pond, which overlooks the old hospital.

It is impressive to see so many large trees in one area. They give you a forest feel in the center of the city. Hang around a while to get the feel of the park, look at the statue of the Civil War general Fitz John Porter, and try out the benches. Relax and think back on your tour of the trees in this historic port city of Portsmouth.

Haven Park

Difficulty rating 2   City traffic. About 3 miles round trip.

1. Douglas Fir

87" CBH   106' VH   36' ACS   Total Points 202 Good Condition
GPS: N 43° 04.542'   W 070° 45.295'
Δ County Champion

2. Horse Chestnut

194" CBH   79' VH   70' ACS   Total Points 291 Good Condition
GPS: N 43° 04.730'   W 070° 45.497'
Δ State Champion

3. European Linden

126" CBH   74' VH   52' ACS   Total Points 213 Good Condition
GPS: N 43° 4.531'   W 070° 45.669'

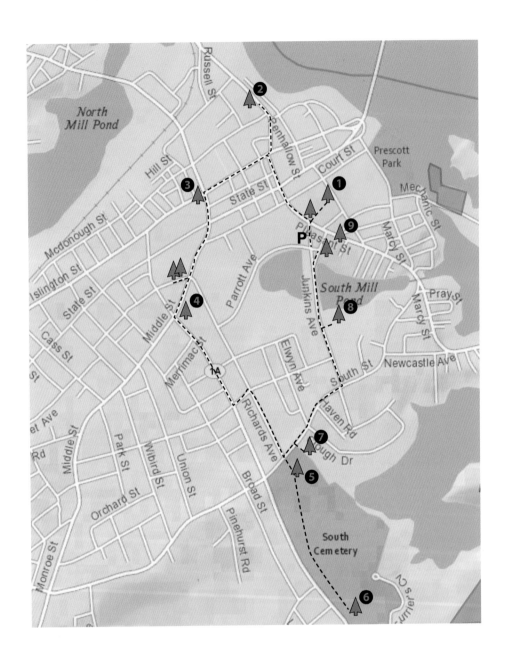

4. European Beech

242" CBH   98' VH   79' ACS   Total Points 360   Excellent Condition
GPS: N 43° 04.273'   W 070° 45.686'
Δ Second largest in the state

5. European Larch

103" CBH   89' VH   46' ACS   Total Points 204   Good Condition
GPS: N 43° 03.947'   W 070° 45.407'
Δ County Champion

6. Norway Spruce

155" CBH   72' VH   40' ACS   Total Points 237   Good Condition
GPS: N 43° 03.733'   W 070° 45.283'

7. Crack Willow

175" CBH   58' VH   40' ACS   Total Points 243   Poor Condition
GPS: N 43° 04.034'   W 070° 45. 374'
Δ County Champion

8. Catalpa

145" CBH   53' VH   47' ACS   Total Points 200   Fair Condition
GPS: N 43° 04.213'   W 070° 45.257'

9. Haven Park Oak

179" CBH   88' VH   59' ACS   Total Points 282   Excellent Condition
GPS: N 43° 04.448'   W 070° 45.258'

Douglas fir
Pseudotsuga menziesii

T he Woodman State Forest in Deerfield is one of the few places in New Hampshire where you will be able to see these West Coast trees growing in some quantity. Many were planted in the 1940s from the state tree nursery in Boscawen, and although I saw only one tree with cones on it, they seem to be reseeding here on their own.

A rare Douglas fir grove in NH

These trees get much larger in their natural habitat, but the short walk to view them here is worth it compared to a flight across the country. A scattered few examples of this type of fir have been planted in some experimental forests and cemeteries across New Hampshire. The former state champion Douglas fir is here along with others similar in size, providing a chance to walk through a grove of them.

The lumber is strong and long lasting and is used in many outdoor applications such as boat keels, deck beams, and piers. It was the wood of choice for the support beams for the long enclosed walkway that was recently rebuilt and goes from a boat docking area to the lighthouse on White Island at the Isles of Shoals, off the coast of New Hampshire.

If you get a chance to see the cones up close, you will notice that they have three pronged bracts coming out from between the scales. It is said to resemble a mouse hiding under the scale with its tail and hind legs hanging out.

Some of the trees may look as though they have a disease that is deteriorating the bark from the ground up, allowing some sort of insect to get into the wood, but foresters will tell you that this is a normal bark change for this type of tree. Some cleanup logging was completed that opened up the woods after a big February windstorm blew over many of the Douglas firs. This logging allows better reseeding in the openings, but nearby trees are more vulnerable to further blow downs, and some of the large specimens have been lost near the edges.

Mouse tail bracts on Douglas fir cone

Clearings have been made farther up the hill in order to encourage the growth of young aspen along with other trees and shrubs that partridge, rabbits, and other wild game are attracted to. I did not notice any wildlife here when I visited in December and wonder what kind of local birds or other wildlife have used the transplanted trees as a source of food and shelter.

Douglas fir trees with different bark stages

Across the dirt road you will notice there have been other species of trees planted at the same time as the firs. The red pines are around in some quantity. If you follow the trail through them, you'll see a quaint little cemetery just over a stonewall with an unusual wood and granite fence surrounding the old gravestones. Back on the dirt road and up the hill on the left, I saw a few red spruce and a good-sized white spruce that have also been planted.

Small cemetery with neat wood and granite fence

Difficulty rating 2

80" CBH   118' VH 34' ACS   Total points 207 Excellent Condition
GPS: N 43° 10.288'   W 071° 11.027'

Directions

From Route 4 in Northwood, take Route 43 for about 1.5 miles and go left on Lower Deerfield Road. Go until the road narrows and crosses a wet area. There is a sign for Woodman Marsh Waterfowl Area on the right. Park there and walk up the hill on the dirt road until you see the tall softwood groves on the right. This area is set aside for hunting, so be safe and wear orange in season.

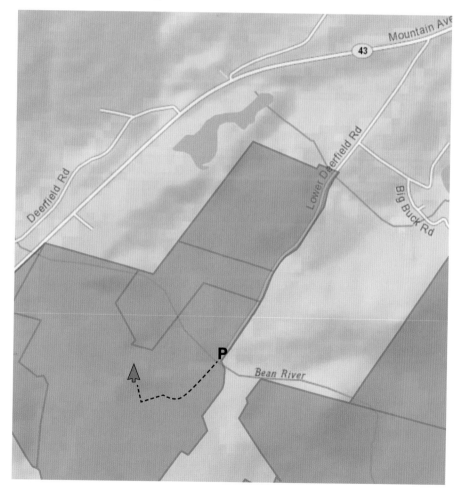

Kingman Farm

T his farm in Madbury was turned over to the University of New Hampshire (UNH) in 1961 and is used for educational and recreational purposes. Extensive trails, used by the public for walking, jogging, biking, snowshoeing, and cross-country skiing, go

This elm has a wild looking top twisting and turning in all directions.

through the property. The Bellamy River flows by the back section, and you'll cross some small feeder streams while on the trails. There are several open fields where the UNH Thompson School's agricultural students experiment with, and learn about, growing new crops. The university has many other properties across the state given to them by alumni of the school. Most are managed as woodlots and are open for recreational use. Some may hold more champion trees.

One of the trees to see here is an American elm on the back part of the property, where its isolation may have helped it escape Dutch elm disease. This one is special in its natural setting on the edge of a wetland. Be sure to stand back and get a good view of the wild-looking crown with the branches twisting and turning every which way. This may be more noticeable with the leaves off. One side of this tree has some decay from water getting in at a fork up high on the trunk. This is common on some large trees where cracks develop as the weight of the

An American elm and Steve Eisenhaure, the forester who cares for UNH owned woodlands across the state.

upper limbs gets to be just too much for the tree to bear. In more open settings, these elms are known for their beauty and graceful, drooping branches and were preferred for planting in town centers or lining driveways up to large estates.

The light-colored wood was once used for barrel hoops and for flooring in barn stables because animal urine would not disintegrate it as quickly as it did other woods. When automobile bodies were made of wood, elm was the choice because its tough fibers held fastenings well. This type of lumber is no longer available at most hardwood retailers but may be occasionally found at small sawmills.

This bigtooth aspen, otherwise known as poplar, is a great specimen of its type, and there are several others nearby to compare it with. Look at these other trees before you get to this state champion to get a better idea of its size. Before its 107-inch girth was measured, the biggest circumference for its type in the state was 88 inches. These fast-growing trees are one of the first to come up after land is cleared, and I assume that the area it is growing in was probably cropland at one time.

There are quite a few invasive barberry plants in the underbrush near these trees, so be prepared for the thorns. No shorts while wandering here! Most aspens are short lived and start deteriorating after about fifty years. Some extraordinary examples like this may reach a hundred or more years in age. Be sure to pick up some of the leaves on the ground and notice the big teeth around the edges. Compared to the quaking aspen, the teeth are quite a bit larger. The yellow autumn leaves look beautiful and hang on until late in the season when most other hardwoods are bare.

The aspens are shade intolerant and are said to be closely associated with the understory that grows around them. In fire-prone areas these are the first trees to grow. The crowns of the young trees are resistant to fire, so crown-burning fires in the conifers will drop to the ground when they reach the aspens. Well known as a favorite food source for partridge (ruffed grouse), these trees are also heavily used by beavers as food and dam building material.

The greenish colored poplar lumber is used for furniture and known as being a very stable secondary wood that is used for the backs and sides of drawers. The Shaker Society commonly used this wood along with pine and maple for furniture as these woods have the simple grain features that their religion prefers.

State champion bigtooth aspen

Difficulty rating 2 to 3 Be sure to wear boots for the wet areas near the elm and tough pants to get through the barberry around the aspens. GPS is required to find the trees.

American Elm

138" CBH 91' VH 82' ACS Total Points 250 Fair Condition

GPS: N 43° 10.475' W 070° 55.530'

Δ State Champion

Bigtooth Aspen

107" CBH 106' VH 54' ACS Total Points 227 Good Condition

GPS: N 43° 10.263' W 070° 55.833'

Δ State Champion

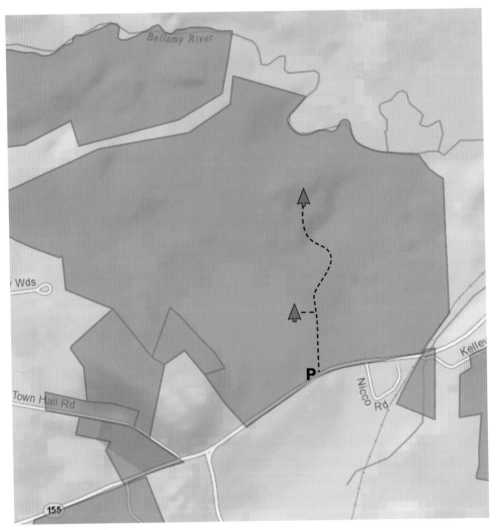

Kingman Farm map

Directions

From Route 4 in Lee, take Route 155 for just under 3 miles. A white house with a red barn on the left is Kingman Farm. Just past the farm is a parking area with a kiosk where the trail starts. From Route 16 in Dover, it is about 2.5 miles in along Route 155 on the right.

Eastern White Pine Tours
Pinus strobes

T his type of pine is probably the most recognized tree in the Northeast, and our state has its share of large ones. In fact the National Champion eastern white pine is in New Hampshire. At 279 inches in circumference, 120 feet high, and 414 total points, it is a significant tree. There are several others close in size throughout the state and some forests with many big pines in them. You will feel dwarfed by these giants when up close to them as they tower high into the sky above you.

The eastern white pine is a very important resource in this part of the country. It was used for boat masts in colonial days, with the tallest specimens marked by the king's agents for British warship masts. Native Americans are known to have medicinal uses for this pine. The Chippewa tribe in the Midwest made a mash using the trunk of a young pine boiled with the bark of wild cherry and wild plum for the treatment of wounds and some forms of rotting flesh. It was reported by tribe members as successful in treating gunshot wounds after gangrene had set in. When sawn the pine lumber is a light and durable wood, excellent for house trim and furniture. Although rarely used for masts anymore, it has its place in boat work as planking for dories and guide boats. Wildlife also benefits from these trees. Tall specimens make good roosting sites for raptors and allow a wide view of the land around them. Squirrels use them for nesting and can pop out of the nest for an easy meal of pinecones when needed.

Bradford Pines

This is a short trail that shows off one of the largest single-stemmed pines in the state. You will see three or four more big pines and hemlocks on the walk along the floodplain of the Warner River. There is a small sign showing you the way to the trail, which brings you across a pedestrian bridge into the woodland. You will start to see some larger trees, and some look impressive, but keep going along the river into the wetter area until at the end you will find the largest of them all. The very top has died so the tree is likely hollow, but you cannot tell from the bottom. This and other trees here are equipped with ground wires to protect them from lightening, which tends to find these highest points in the landscape. I found an eagle feather on the ground near the base of the tree when I came in the summer. I would assume that eagles roost in this tree, so we can associate this pine with the bald eagle.

The biggest of the Bradford Pines

This is a scenic and laid-back part of the state. I am sure you can find other things to fill out your day after this short walk. Lake Massasecum is not far off and has a campground and swimming beach. Sunapee State Park, with its hiking trails, lake access, and downhill skiing, is nearby in Newbury.

Difficulty rating 1 Could be wet in the spring

180" CBH 132' VH 35' ACS Total points 321 Good condition

GPS: N 43° 15.974' W 071° 57.588'

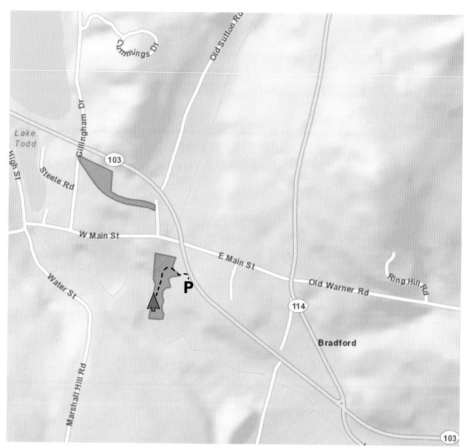

Bradford Pines

Directions

Take Route 89 to exit 9 in Warner. Follow Route 103 toward Bradford and Newbury. When you get into Bradford, go about a half-mile after the junction with Rte 114 to a roadside pullover on the left. There is no clear entrance to the trail, so you will have to search a little. The trail starts about 100 feet north, or toward town, from the parking area, across the grassy road buffer.

College Woods Durham

This property has been a staple of the University of New Hampshire (UNH) forestry school since its early years. It is managed for many wood species and used as an outdoor classroom for thousands of students. There are trails all through the woods that are used daily by walkers and joggers and connect to the Field House area at the school. The total size is about 230 acres with 60 acres set aside in 1961 as a natural area not to be cut. The hurricanes of 1938 and 1954 left their mark here; the winds took down some of the large trees, but many survived to this day.

When walking here you will see a good number of those very large and tall trees. One tree nicknamed the Paul Bunyan Pine was well known among the UNH alumni. The top had snapped off in a windstorm in 2003, but you can still see the hulking stump of the pine and get an idea of why it had that name.

Difficulty rating 1 to 2

148" CBH 114' VH 50' ACS Total points 275 Good condition
GPS: N 43° 08.216' W 070° 56.718'

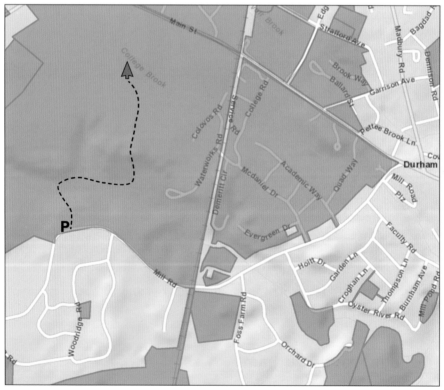

College Woods Durham

Directions

Take Route 108 into the center of Durham and go around to the one-way section bearing left back toward the downtown area. Take a right onto Mill Road and pass the DUMP (Durham Market Place) on the left. Go about a mile, and just past Woodbridge Road look for a pullover at the curve on the right side. Park here or you can find a few more trail access points at other spots along the side of the road. The trail will bring you over the Oyster River into the woods with several paths through them. Trail maps are available online, at the UNH Woodlands website. The featured trees at college woods are hard to find without a GPS but there are many similar trees all along the trails.

Tamworth Pines

This is a great hike into the edge of the White Mountains near the Hemmingway State Forest. You drive along a road called the Chinook Trail, which leads to a famous kennel farther up the road where sled dogs were trained for Admiral Byrd's Antarctic expeditions and Army Search and Rescue units.

You start the hike at a sign for the Big Pines Natural Area, which is maintained by the Tamworth Conservation Commission. Go down the trail and cross the bridge over the Swift River to the trail loop sign and go left, as they encourage you to go. This way you can keep wondering if the large tree you are seeing is the right one or not. You will know it when you finally come to the biggest.

The loop trail starts out along the edge of the steep riverbank, with the noise of the rapids as company. Along the top of the ravine you start bearing right and see some tall trees along the way. This is a prime example of how trees can grow tall and clear in a hillside setting. You will pass the trail up to the Great Hill fire tower and could add that on to the trip if you like. Many of these pines you are passing are over 10 feet in circumference. The biggest pine you come to is among the tallest in the state at 148 feet.

On your way down and back to the river, you will notice how damp the air is with the river and streams flowing through here off the hills. The moisture seems to hold and collect, giving that rain forest feel. Maybe that is what helped these trees reach their great size.

This is the biggest pine in the impressive Big Pines Natural Area.

Besides the trees, it is well worth a trip to this part of New Hampshire. Be sure to stop in Tamworth. It is an interesting small town with the Remick Museum and the Barnstormers Theatre as cultural attractions.

Difficulty rating 3

179" CBH   148' VH 51' ACS   Total points 340   Good condition
GPS: N 43° 53.047'   W 071° 17.71'

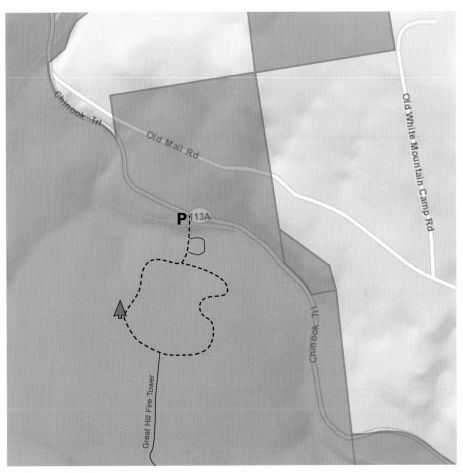

Tamworth Pines

Directions

From Route 16 take Route 113 in Chocorua. At just over 2 miles take a right onto 113a, called the Chinook Highway, in Tamworth. About 2.5 miles from the start of the road, park on the left side where there is a small sign for Big Pines Natural Area. Trail maps may be available there, or they can be printed online. Cross the bridge and take the loop by going left.

Northern New Hampshire

White Mountain Lumber in Berlin

Berlin Test Nursery

The Kelley family of White Mountain Lumber owns land on the east side of the Androscoggin River in Berlin and runs the lumberyard there. The back lot has an unusual variety of trees that were planted by the former paper plant owners, the Brown Company, as a test nursery. They tested many types of European tree species here to see how well they grew and then planted seedlings at their nursery farm on the shores of Cupsuptic Lake in Maine to sell to the landscaping trade.

The trees still growing at this test site included Scotch pine, Austrian pine, mugo pine, and Norway spruce. You will also find some native white cedar and balsam fir. Barry Kelley and other family members are kind enough to allow access to the land so we can see a few champions of these species.

The trip takes you along nice wide paths through these foreign trees and onto the edge of a farmhouse field. You can park along the side of the road just past the lumberyard or, if in the winter, up near the water treatment plant. Enter the woods at a chained entry road into the property near a small cemetery.

The mugo pines are near the far end of the plantings and will not impress you with their size. Notice, though, that the bark is a bit different and the branches in some areas curl at the ends. Also called Swiss pine, these are a high-elevation species that do not grow very tall and can be trimmed into low, full-foliaged landscape ornamentals. Their large native range makes the tree somewhat unpredictable in size because it has adapted to the many climates in most of Europe and western Asia. The spelling of the tree's name was said to be botched in some early encyclopedias, and that spelling as mugho pine is shown on the landscape name tags from the 1930s that they still have at White Mountain Lumber.

Keep going to find the state champion Scotch (also called Scots) pine over near the road. There are two here that are considerably larger than others seen in plantations in the southern part of the state. The tops have a beige-orange bark, making them easy to identify. They are known to have poor growth habits in this country because pine grosbeaks, along with some insects, feed on the terminal buds and cause the tops to grow crooked. This species is grown mostly for sale as Christmas trees or as an ornamental.

Tree labels of copper wire and wood from the 1930s

Next you should see the balsam fir, which is natural for the area and has the coarse bark of the older trees. This species is common in the northern part of New Hampshire and is the most abundant tree in Maine. The tops of these trees tend to form a spire that stands out among all others. Younger trees have smooth bark with blisters that hold a resin called Canada balsam. Some Native Americans used this resin mixed with bear grease as an external treatment for headaches. If you brush up against the branches, you can easily smell the fragrance of the needles. These needles are packed in small pillows and sold as aromatic satchels all over the world.

These Austrian pines line the side of the trail.

The balsam fir is the quintessential Christmas tree of the Northeast, and the smell is well known by most in New England as a sign of the holiday season. In the winter the trees are an important food source for deer and moose. The cones turn dark purple and grow upright instead of hanging down like the cones on most other conifers. The lumber is used for building construction and is sold in the Northeast under the spruce-pine-fir type. It is also used for pulpwood.

The last tree to find here is the Austrian pine, also called black pine. Originally from Austria and Yugoslavia, these trees have been planted extensively in the United States as an ornamental. It is known to be adaptable to many soil conditions and is salt spray tolerant. These features make this one of the few pines suited for urban conditions. Hundreds of thousands were planted in the Midwest as windbreaks after the drought in the Dust Bowl area killed many native species. This is an appealing tree that is rarely found in a New Hampshire woodland setting like you see here.

Difficulty rating 1

1. Scotch Pine

110" CBH   84' VH   38' ACS   Total Points 204   Excellent Condition
GPS: N 44° 30.229'   W 071° 09.304'
Δ State Champion

2. Mugo Pine

36" CBH   56' VH   19' ACS   Total Points 97   Excellent Condition
GPS: N 44° 30.313'   W 071° 09.257'
Δ State Champion

3. Balsam Fir

58" CBH   97' VH   21' ACS   Total Points 160   Excellent Condition
GPS: N 44° 30.219'   W 071° 09.238'
Δ State Co-Champion

4. Austrian Pine

69" CBH   81' VH   33' ACS   Total Points 158   Excellent Condition
GPS: N 44° 30.156'   W 071° 09.251'
Δ State Champion

Directions

Take Route 16 into Berlin and cross the river on the right over the 12th Street Bridge. Take a left at the intersection on Hutchins Street, which changes its name to East Milan Road. Go about half a mile and park on the side of the road just past White Mountain Lumber.

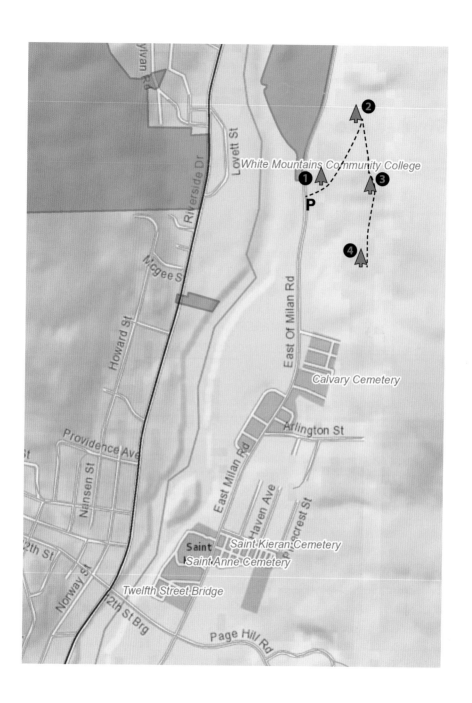

Snyder Brook

T ake this hike toward the Presidential Range if you want to see some of the best old growth trees in the state. Many of these are growing along a mountain brook with several waterfalls, which add to the beauty of this section of the White Mountain National Forest. The hemlocks here will wow you with their old look and grand size. Some of these trees have been dated to 370 years old. Thirty-six acres of this land was bought by the Appalachian Mountain Club (AMC) in 1895 to protect the scenic area from the extensive logging that was going on at the time. The parcel was turned over to become part of the national forest in the 1930s.When starting from the parking area, check out the kiosk map to get oriented. Head past the power lines to where the signs direct you to Valley Way and then on to the Maple Walk Trail.

The first tree to find is the biggest American beech in Coos County about 75 feet off the trail on your left. The beech is on the bank of Snyder Brook and likely attracts the attention of many animals that follow the brook. The beechnut is an important food source for all sizes of wildlife, from chipmunks to bears. The beech tree has smooth bark when young, but most old trees now have beech bark disease, which causes cankers and roughens the bark. I have no experience using beech lumber. It is now used mostly for pulpwood and firewood. In the past it was used for furniture, clothespins, and other woodenware. In Europe there were once workers called beech bodgers, whose sole job was to split beech bolts (short round sections of a log) and shave them into dowels for chair legs and backs.

Keep going on the path to where it meets Fallsway Trail and continues along Snyder Brook. You will start seeing some older-looking hemlocks of increasing size. Many have the characteristic chunky bark of old growth, and two of them measure out to be tied for the largest in Coos County. There are bigger hemlocks in the state, but the old growth

One of several waterfalls in the area

Checking the circumference of the state champion red spruce

look and the number of big hemlocks here, along with the beautiful waterfalls in the brook, will leave you feeling humbled by nature's wonder.

Nearby you will see a few conifer trees that have smoother bark than the hemlocks, and thin reddish brown scales. These are red spruce. The state champion is here, and it will impress you with its long, clear trunk. This species thrives in well-drained rocky soil and likes the north side of mountain slopes, where it will often grow in pure stands. The dark green needles are prickly to the touch and point toward the tip of the branch.

I have used the lumber for floor joists and wall studs as this is the most common wood sawn for the building trade. I have also used it for canoe gunwales and deck beams, and it makes nice lightweight canoe paddles or rowing oars.

Difficulty rating 2

1. American Beech

94" CBH   83' VH   41' ACS   Total Points 187   Good Condition
GPS: N 44° 22.140'   W 071° 17.230'
Δ **Coos County Champion**

2 & 3. Eastern Hemlock

122" CBH   87' VH   39' ACS   Total Points 219   Excellent Condition
GPS: N 44° 22.011'   W 071° 17.227'
Δ **Coos County Co-Champions both here**

4. Red Spruce

96" CBH   86' VH   36' ACS   Total Points 191 Excellent Condition
GPS: N 44° 21.937'   W 071° 17.258'
Δ **State Champion**

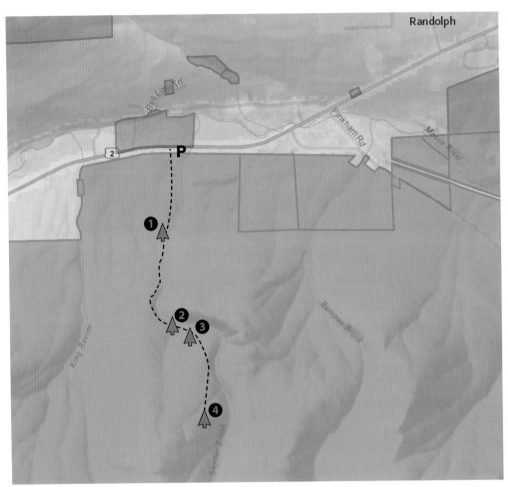

Snyder Brook

Directions

To get to Snyder Brook, drive on Route 2 from Lancaster or Gorham and go to the Appalachia parking area in Randolph. This is about 5 miles from the Route 16 junction in Gorham or about 18 miles from Route 3 in Lancaster. Park in the hikers' parking area on the south side of the road and follow the trail signs to Valley Way.

Yellow Birch
Betula alleghaniensis

If you want to see a large yellow birch that is in its prime, then this is the one to see. It is a mountain trip bringing you to Crawford Notch in the New Hampshire White Mountains. Crawford Notch is named after the family that settled here and built what ended up as a grand hotel, the Crawford House, to accommodate tourists coming to the area. The vacant hotel burned down in 1977 and the Appalachian Mountain Club now operates the Highland Center at the same site. There are many interesting historical stops and trails leading to natural features all through the notch. So allow some extra time here before or after viewing the tree.

Fall foliage at Crawford Notch

Yellow birch in its prime

The birch is off the Dry River Trail not far in from the road. A continuation hike could be taken from here farther into the mountains if desired. From the trail this birch could be passed by, but when you get close you realize what a nice example it is. The wide girth is impressive and its thick plating bark stands out. On younger trees the bark is smoother and peels with small curls like the bark of paper birch, but the color is more of a yellowish brown or silver. On older trees like this one, the bark has a gray or black color. The roots crawl over the rocky ground searching for good soil and water in this harsh mountain landscape.

The lumber of this species is the most sought after of all the birches and is the most expensive. It is used for furniture, cabinets, interior doors, and woodenware. The wood has a reddish color, and the tight grain allows for a good finish when varnished. Although I did not notice any wildlife associated with this tree, it is commonly browsed on by moose and deer. Snowshoe hare and partridge eat the seeds, catkins, and buds.

Difficulty rating 2

106" CBH 80' VH 57' ACS   Total points 200 Excellent condition
GPS: N 44° 09.679   W 071° 21.828'

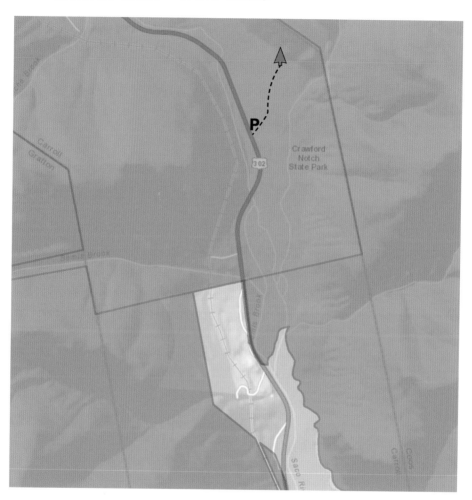

Directions

To get there, take Route 302 from North Conway straight through Bart-
lett and into Crawford Notch. Just past the Dry River Campground,
look for a small pullover for the Dry River Trail. The tree is several hundred feet up the trail on the left. The Dry River Trail farther in was
closed in 2012, so obey any signs that warn of going farther.

How to Tell the Age of a Big Tree

One of the most common questions asked in the Big Tree Program is "How old do you think the tree is?" This is usually difficult to answer because there are so many reasons why some trees are bigger than others. When I built my house in 1979, there were many trees left growing around the house and two red oaks near where the garden was put in. We cleared some trees for the garden and there was an oak about a foot in diameter next to the clearing and a smaller oak behind it with other trees nearby.

As time went on, the oak near the garden grew steadily while the smaller tree growing in its shade stayed about the same size. About twenty-five years later, I cut them both to make more room for the garden, and the bigger tree was over 24 inches in diameter and the other maybe 10 inches in diameter. I counted the growth rings and was amazed that they were the same age. One just had more sunlight and fertilizer available to it, so it grew much larger.

When trying to determine a tree's age, it is always best to look at the history of the area in which it is growing. If it's in the front or back yard of an older home and is a different type of tree than one that grows naturally in the area, then I would assume that your tree (perhaps a Norway spruce or a European beech) was planted as an ornamental around the time the house was built. Even some of the local native trees were likely left as shade trees when the house was built. If you find out when the home was constructed, then you'll likely have an idea of the age of your tree.

It's more difficult to determine the age of a tree in a forest, but you can sometimes tell by when the land was last logged over or if the land had been used as a pasture for sheep. Some of the trees that are now large were left back then as shade trees for the livestock or as seed trees in a newly cut forest. If your big oak is along a stonewall or a property boundary, you can check your deed and see if it is noted as a boundary tree.

One surefire way to tell is to have a core sample taken and the growth rings counted, but that is not really necessary unless you may have a very old or unusual tree that could have some scientific or historical significance. Many older trees that have heart rot cannot be cored for age because the center is gone. There is also concern by some that taking a core makes the tree more vulnerable to diseases introduced through the hole or even by the coring equipment. Just keep in mind that some of our oldest trees are small and misshapen, having grown in a difficult environment where the human hand has had a hard time getting to them and may have been subject to diseases or fires. Big trees do not necessarily mean old trees.

Forest Lake State Park

You will find several large trees in this North Country park. One of the ten original state parks developed in 1935, Forest Lake State Park consists of 397 acres of woodlands and a 200-foot-long sandy beach. In the summer the lake is enjoyed by many of the local families and would allow a nice swim to cool off after your journey through these woods.

On this venture you will seek out an ash, a wonderful paper birch, and several large oaks. They are growing on the side and near the top of Dalton Mountain. You will need to walk into the forest off any trails to find the Big Trees, and a GPS will be necessary. On the way in there was quite a bit of raspberry and blackberry growth in the old logging roads,

This stone fireplace is all that is left of a ski shelter.

Retired Coos County forester Sam Stoddard with county champion paper birch

making the walk difficult, but we took a better way out and avoided them for the most part.

The first tree to go to is the largest white ash in Coos County. It may not last too much longer as the center has rotted most of the way up the tree, with the only live wood holding up the tree along the outer edge near the bark. Insects will find their way to the rotting wood, and many birds and small animals will chip away at the tree to feed on the insects. Some larger animal may come by and tear the wood apart even more looking for ants and grubs till the tree eventually will fall over and further decay takes place on the ground.

Not too far off you will see a Big Oak and then another close by that one. These are old, expansive trees with wide spreading branches. There was an old pasture here where the army raised mules during WW1. The trees grew on the edges of the former opening or were left as shade trees, which allowed them to gain size. Then the pasture filled in with the younger trees that are all around now. There are remnants of old stonewalls, a well, and a fireplace not too far off. The fireplace was in an open-faced shelter that was used by skiers when ski trails followed the slopes. There is a shelter still standing lower down on the slopes that you could search for if you like.

The must-see tree for this trip is the paper birch. Commonly known as the white birch, or long ago as canoe birch, this example is what the Native Americans would search out. They would remove the bark for many uses, such as canoes, bowls, packs and so forth. This is a healthy-looking tree that should keep gaining in size. It is the third largest in the state but in better condition than the other two, so as long as it doesn't fall over from the lean it has, it could gain on its status.

I associate all these trees with the moose because we saw one here while we were finding the way out. It seemed content to block our way and kept looking off to the side, where we heard another moose crashing in the brush. We decided that a wide berth around them was our best bet. On any of these hikes, be sure to give any large wildlife plenty of room and they will likely ignore you or run off.

1. White Ash

131" CBH   72' VH   39' ACS   Total points 213   Poor condition
GPS: N 44° 21.696'   W 071° 41.781'
Δ Coos Champ

2. Red Oak 1

182" CBH   91' VH   59' ACS   Total points 288   Good condition
GPS: N 44° 21.661'   W 071° 41.801'
Δ Coos Co-Champ with oak below

3. Red Oak 2

191" CBH   77' VH   66' ACS   Total points 285   Good condition
GPS: N 44° 21.680'   W 071° 41.808'
Δ Coos Co-Champ

4. Paper Birch

104" CBH   80' VH   51' ACS   Total points 197   Good condition
GPS: N 44° 21.617'   W 071° 41.828'
Δ Coos Champ

Difficulty rating 3 to 4 Trees some distance off trail; some thorn bushes may be in tote roads. GPS required.

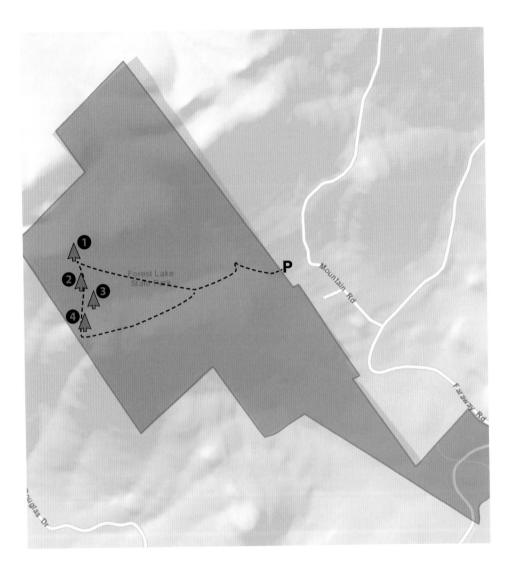

Directions

Off Route 142 take Forest Lake Road and go right onto Faraway Road. Then go left onto Mountain Road. About a quarter mile up at a sharp curve in the road, there is a grassy access road to the antenna buildings. Go straight in and park out of the way near the building so the crew can access the building if need be while you are hiking. Walk down the unmarked trail, and at a fork go left and off to the trees. GPS for parking is N 44° 21.760' W 071° 41.073'.

Forest Lake Park oak

Northern White Cedar
Thuja occidentalis

Ahh, this is one of my favorite trees. I use the wood often for boat and canoe planking and for ribs in wood-canvas canoes. It smells great when I pull the freshly steamed ribs out of the steam box and bend them around a form. This species does not grow naturally near me, so when I need some there is always a journey involved to some faraway small sawmill in cedar country.

The Clarksville cedars trip will be one to remember, with its long drive along the dirt roads around a wilderness lake where the land is managed for its lumber resource. Lake Francis was windswept with small whitecaps as we went by, adding to the wild feel of the day. There was a cold bite to the air in mid October, some of the hardwoods still had color, and the tamaracks were showing their golden needles.

View to First Connecticut Lake and Prospect Mountain

When you park, the walk will bring you down from the hardwood upland right to the edge of the softwood swamp where the cedars are. These cedars are the largest in the state of New Hampshire, and there are three here very close in size. Although I did not see a bear on the trip, I have to associate these trees with the black bear. All the big cedars here have great wear on the trunks from years of territorial marking by the black bears in the area. The aromatic wood attracts the bears, and they seem to prefer the cedar over other nearby trees. To mark their part of the world, these big animals stand on their hind legs and reach as high as they can, then claw and bite the trees. They will rub their scent all over the trunk also. Wandering bears coming into the area can recognize the scent and see how high the marks are to determine if they dare come into the territory. Bears are naturally wary of humans, and if you do see one it will most likely be scampering away in the woods. If you come across one that does not run away, keep your distance and use all safety precautions as described by New Hampshire Fish and Game.

The white cedar trees at this site are enormous and pleasant to be around. The bark that is left feels smooth and soft, as does the foliage. The ground around them is also soft for the most part, and

State champion northern white cedar

even though it is a little wet, it all feels comfortable. The cedars are valuable to wildlife, and we humans have found many uses for them. The small cones provide food for birds and red squirrels while deer and moose will browse on the twigs. A tea made from the bark and leaves has saved many a life of the scurvy-ridden colonists when they arrived in this country.

Talk about long lived, I just read about a recent study where a researcher scaled down a cliff to some twisted, gnarly-looking cedars, took some core samples, and found that the trees were over a thousand years old. Studies have also shown how decay resistant the white cedar is; researchers found sound wood from a tree that died 3,550 years ago. Even more amazing is that submerged cedar was pulled up from Georgian Bay in Ontario that was dated to 8,500 years ago, and the wood was still in good condition.

While traveling in northern New Hampshire, keep in mind that there is a proud logging heritage in this area. The land is managed for the type of wood that is needed to provide an income for the locals and the landowners. Conservation easements are in place that have in mind the needs of wildlife and keep the land open for hunters, fishermen, hikers, boaters, and tree searchers like us. This was never farmland up here; it

Black bear territorial marks on this big cedar

State champion yellow birch

has always been a working forest. The acreage these cedars are on is part of a 23,000-acre parcel owned by New Hampshire Fish and Game. This and the neighboring land is former paper company property, now owned by Fish and Game and a private investment firm. An agreement was worked out that keeps the private portion consisting of about 140,000 acres undeveloped, with the forestland sustainably managed by a local forest consulting firm. The state maintains the roads so the public can use them, and the roads provide access to the forests for logging and management needs. Be sure to keep an eye out for logging trucks that could come around a corner with a full load at any time. The roads are narrow and the trucks cannot stop easily, so you should be ready to give them plenty of room so they can get by.

A yellow birch is nearby that was not seen when the cedars were first found, and it has measured out to be the new state champion. It is a very large tree with some hollowing in the center. It may be hidden if there are leaves on the small trees surrounding the moss-covered beast. Be sure to check out the young beech on the way out of these woods. Some have claw marks from the bears climbing up after the beechnuts.

Difficulty rating 4   Be sure to take GPS and compass readings to get to the trees and to get back to your vehicle.

Northern White Cedars

#1: 132" CBH   83' VH   29' ACS   223 Total points   Good condition

GPS: N 45° 01.898'   W 071° 15.026'
Δ State Co-Champion

#2: 129" CBH 89' VH 28' ACS   225 Total points   Good condition

GPS: N 45° 01.938'   W 071° 14.991'
Δ State Co-Champion

Yellow Birch

152" CBH   87' VH   51' ACS   Total points 242   Good condition

GPS: N 45° 01.938'   W 071° 15.003'
Δ State Champion

Directions

To get to these trees, take Route 3 into Pittsburg, turn right onto Route 145 or Mill Road, and take your first left onto appropriately named Cedar Stream Road. You will go by the berm for the Lake Francis Dam and then cross a stream. Follow the edge of the lake about 4.5 miles.

After the road leaves the lakeshore go about 2 more miles and bear left at a fork through the gate. Go 1/4 mile and take a left at #9 and go over the stream at gate 199. Even if the gates are closed you are close enough that you can park there and head out to the tree, otherwise follow Bog Branch Road 1 to 1.5 miles and look for a place to pull over. If you come to a clearing with a nice view of First Connecticut Lake, you have gone too far.

Note: these roads can be closed for mud season in the early spring or for other reasons. Road closures are listed on the New Hampshire State Parks website, nhstatepark.org. Look up "Connecticut Lakes Headwaters" under parks listings and then go to road closures to find gate numbers and road names. The gate numbers can be changed so you may have to go by the road name.

Once you park your car, you are on your own as there is no clear trail. Go through the woods and look for a very old tote road that tends to go to the north. The cedars are near the edge of this road.

GPS for parking: N 45° 01.592' W 071° 14.804'

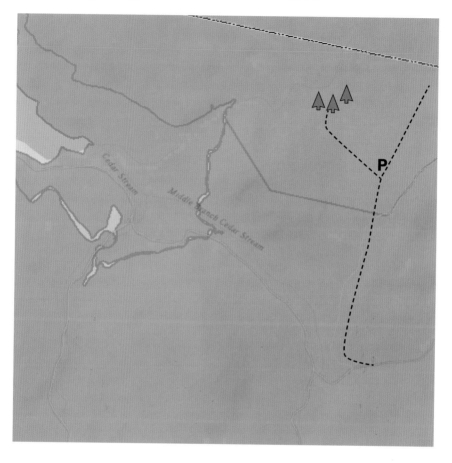

Black Spruce
Picea mariana

T he trail to Mud Pond is handicap accessible for those who have trouble getting around. Do not let that keep out the more able bodied though. I enjoyed the trail and boardwalk that brings you through some young balsam firs and into a black spruce-white cedar seepage swamp and finally out to Mud Pond. This is all part of the Pondicherry Refuge. The trail was built by volunteers from the Friends of Pondicherry group, who enlisted the help of the Youth Conservation Corp to thin the trees and make the trail and boardwalk.

Mud Pond boardwalk

On the way in there are several rock rest stops and benches along the trail to sit and view the many birds at this site. Mosses and orchids are abundant in the swamp and in the fen near the pond. There is a rather small black spruce near a bench on the left side of the boardwalk on your way in, and you should examine it carefully for identification purposes. It was a county champion but was beaten out in size by the new National Champion black spruce nearby in another part of the refuge. I was told to consider the species as the lollipop tree because under some conditions it has a long slender stem with full branches and needles at the very top, while the similar red spruce is full all the way up. There is also a subtle color difference, with black spruce having darker bark and bluer needles than red spruce.

Black spruce is used for construction lumber and pulpwood. I have not knowingly used it myself, although it could be mixed with standard construction-grade spruce-pine-fir that I buy at times.

The boardwalk ends at an outlook over the pond and fen. A bog has no outlet, while a fen like this has a drainage stream. Here we saw hooded mergansers and gray jays along with many other birds. The whole Pondicherry Refuge is a bird-watcher's dream in the fall or spring during migration. A trail guide is available and provides more information about this wonderful wildlife hotspot. There are not many Big Trees at Mud Pond, but it's a great spot to visit while in the area.

No tree measurements or coordinates. Just bring a tree identification book along with a birding book and have fun.

Handicap accessible.

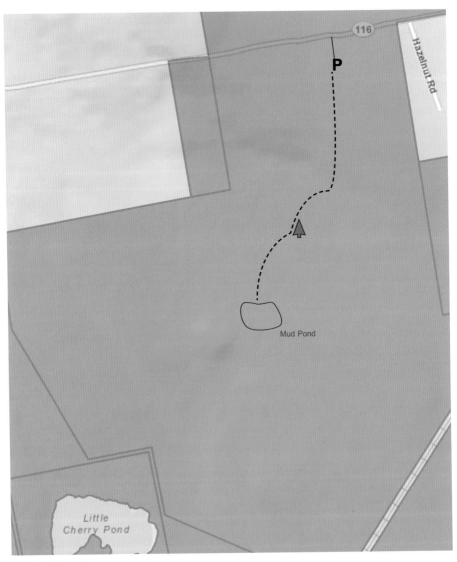

Mud Pond

Directions

From Route 3 in Whitefield, take Route 116 about 6 miles to the trailhead to Mud Pond on the right.

Pondicherry National Wildlife Refuge

D riving into this reserve, you will be impressed by the big country view of the Presidential Range and other mountain ranges rising out of the valley. They seem to always be in the background providing grand views wherever you go. This is an easy trail starting in Whitefield, going in about 1.7 miles along an abandoned railroad bed, and ending up in Jefferson, New Hampshire. The trip will take you into Cherry Pond with one of the best mountain views in the state, then off the main trail and through the spruce, fir, and tamarack woods to Little Cherry Pond. Along the way you will see a few county champion trees, a state champ, and the National Champion black spruce. The first tree to see is the white spruce, about a quarter mile in on the right and about sixty feet or so off the trail just over a wire fence. Some smaller trees have been removed in the immediate area to allow a nice view of this state champion spruce. You can notice the fuller foliage from the ground up and the very light gray bark, which differentiates the white spruce from the other spruces. White spruce also can get considerably larger than red or black spruce.

Spruce has many uses in the building of boats. The lumber is light in weight and strong, and holds fastenings much better than pine or cedar. I use it for things such as gunwales, deck beams, and carlins, where lighter wood is important but screws or nails must hold well. If the tree is cut about three feet above the ground, the trunk and roots can be dug out and re-sawn for ribs and stems in Adirondack guide boats. These trees are also a source of the 2 by 4s and dimensional lumber used in building houses and other buildings.

Keep going on the main trail down past some power lines and then to Cherry Pond. Take a side trip over to the viewing platform on the right where a sign directs you toward it. What a view. In the winter it is definitely a white wonderland, and the spring or fall will offer bird-watchers a treat with many kinds of birds migrating through the reserve.

View of Mt. Washington from the outlet of Cherry Pond

State champion white spruce and Dave Govatski

Go back to the main trail and keep an eye out for the trail sign to Little Cherry Pond. There is another sign on the Coos County champ gray birch saying that this is a wildlife preserve owned by the New Hampshire Audubon Society. Audubon owns the land around both the Cherry Ponds, and classifies this as an important birding area in New Hampshire.

The gray birch is known as a pioneer species as it is one of the first to venture into new clearings or burns. It is often seen in clumps of several trees together. When a breeze blows through them, the leaves quake the way poplar leaves (quaking aspen) do—hence their scientific name, Betula populifolia, meaning birch with poplar leaves. The species is thought of as temporary, just holding a spot for the more permanent forests that will come after. Gray birch are short lived so do not get large; they are used for pulpwood (for making paper) and for firewood.

It will feel good to get off the wide railroad tracks and on this narrow woods trail. About 600 feet in after passing a good-sized balsam fir, start looking for the National Champion black spruce on the left about fifty feet off the trail. It is quite tall and very healthy looking but not what you may expect to see for the biggest of its type in the United States. This is an example of why it is important to look at other trees while on the trips in this book. As you see many examples of a certain kind of tree, you will learn to appreciate the champions more, even the ones that do not grow to a giant size.

Farther into the woods, your GPS may tell you that you are at the bigtooth aspen, but after looking around a bit you likely will not see it. There should be some red flags on the trees to your right, and if you follow them a hundred feet or so they will bring you to the tree. If you visit in the late fall, you will notice the tops of the aspens rippling in the breeze with their nice yellow color among the nearby greens of the softwoods. Commonly known as poplar, the lumber from the species is available at retail lumberyards and small sawmills.

It is not much farther to Little Cherry Pond, so keep going through these fine northern woods. You will pass some pure spruce groves and then all balsam fir, with their spire-like tops. Finally after some blow downs when you are almost at the pond, you will see some small tamarack, also called American larch.

Difficulty rating 2

1. White Spruce

108" CBH   98' VH   39' ACS   Total Points 216   Good Condition
GPS: N 44° 21.706'   W 71° 32.030'
Δ State Champion

2. Gray Birch

56" CBH   62' VH   19' ACS   Total Points 123   Fair Condition
GPS: N 44° 22.650'   W 071° 31.063'
Δ County Champion

3. Black Spruce

71" CBH   93' VH   35' ACS   Total Points 173   Excellent Condition
GPS: N 44° 22.642'   W 071° 31.208'
Δ National Champion

4. Bigtooth Aspen

68" CBH   93' VH   37' ACS   Total Points 170   Excellent Condition
GPS: N 44° 22.637'   W 071° 31.364'
Δ County Champion

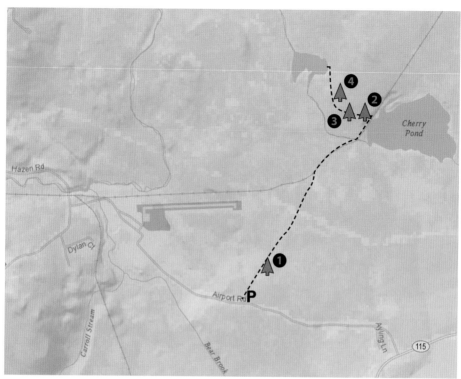

Pondicherry National Wildlife Refuge

Directions

Get on Route 115 that goes from Route 3 in Carroll to Route 2 in Jefferson. About 4 to 5 miles (halfway) in, take Hazen Road and go in 1.5 miles to the parking area for the Pondicherry Wildlife Refuge on the right. Drive across the bridge to the kiosk and park.

Mountain paper birch

Mountain Paper Birch
Betula cordifolia Regal

Jefferson Notch Road, the highest state highway in New Hampshire, will bring you just over 3,000 feet in elevation near the site of this mountain dweller. This is not the same tree as the regular paper birch, and you should be able to notice some slight differences. The bark has a more salmon-colored tinge to it and is shaggier than the bark of the regular paper birch. The leaves are heart shaped, which distinguishes this from the other birches, and this species lives longer than the others. You will find them either along jagged coastlines or in the mountains, as seen here. They are listed as a different species than paper birch in many tree books, while others consider it as just another variety of the paper birch. Some leading foresters and botanists recognize this as quite different from the paper birch in its leaf shape and habitat so would like to see it classified as a separate species.

The drive itself is an adventurous ride into the Presidential Range of the White Mountains. The narrow dirt road is several miles long and closed in the winter. There are few places to pull over until you get to the high point with views of Mount Washington and a parking area for the Caps Ridge Trail.

There was a fresh dusting of snow on the trees when we started up the mountain trail in mid October. You will find the tree a few hundred feet up to the left of the trail. Just look for the largest birch, as there are many birches mixed in with the red spruce and balsam fir.

After you spend some time looking over this rugged high country birch, you should consider going farther up the trail to see some of the large rocks with potholes in them. The potholes are from the river water than ran over ledges and left small stones swirling in areas, where they wore down the rock and caused the holes. This all happened thousands of years ago, down in the valley, when the glaciers scoured the valley floor and deposited them up here on the trail. There is a nice view of

Mt. Washington from the Caps Ridge parking area

the mountains from the rocks, but be aware that it is a steep climb of about one mile to them. If you are up to it, keep going to get to some of the highest mountaintops of New Hampshire.

Difficulty rating 3   Mostly because of the long, winding dirt road up the mountain

63" CBH   48' VH   32' ACS   Total Points 119   Fair condition
GPS coordinates: N 44° 17.787'   W 71° 21.040'
Δ **State Champion**

Directions

From the junction of Routes 2 and 115 in Jefferson, go about 1.4 miles and take a left on Valley Road. Go just under 3 miles and turn right onto the Jefferson Notch Road. Note that it is not open in the winter. Call the Forest Service for the closing dates. Go just over 5 miles to the parking lot at Caps Ridge trailhead, the highest point on the road.

Avoid the road in heavy rains or ice storms. This is a winding, narrow dirt road that brings you up into the mountains. Be sure to keep an eye out for cars coming the other way.

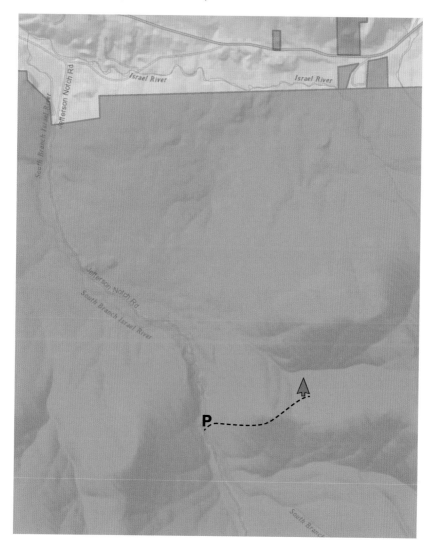

Caring for Big Trees

These special Big Trees also need special care. The NH Arborists Association will tell us that they are not to be pruned and cared for the same way as smaller versions. The heavy branches may benefit from a support system comprised of cables and/or brace rods if structural weaknesses are present. If the trees are in the woods like many of those in this book are, the lower branches are likely getting shaded by the growing forest around the tree. One time this may have been a pasture and the oak tree was thriving with its branches stout and strong but now the lower part of the tree is shaded too much and those branches are likely dying and falling off. Special care needs to be taken to be sure productive branches that do reach the sun are not pruned and the dead lower stubs are cut in a manner that allows the wound to heal properly.

Big Trees provide big benefits to our cities and towns.

Trees in the cities that could be near homes may be pruned for other reasons. A branch may be hovering over a house, or too close to the roads or power lines where trimming for clearance is needed. When thinning for the overall health of the tree, care must be taken to ensure the limbs that are providing the most benefit to the tree are not cut. There is more competition and less natural nutrients available when grass or sidewalks are nearby, so thoughtful fertilization may improve health. This can vary for each species of tree and a certified arborist should be consulted before any work is done. If care is provided to industry standards, a tree's safe and useful life expectancy can be protected and extended.

It has been shown that in an urban environment the large trees are much more cost effective than the smaller trees. They provide more shade, which keeps cooling costs down and increases the time between resurfacing of roads. They reduce storm water runoff and contribute to improving the quality of our air and water. They also provide wildlife habitat, increase property values and make a community much more attractive. This value far out-weighs the costs for care and maintenance of these giant assets in our cities and towns.

Western New Hampshire

Walpole

You will find many groves of larch planted at the Fox State Forest.

Fox State Forest

In 1922 Miss Carolyn A. Fox donated her home and the land around it to the state of New Hampshire along with a substantial trust fund to use for forestry research. Dr. Henry Baldwin was hired as the first research forester in 1933, and he lived and worked out of the home. Considered one of the giants of early New Hampshire forestry, Dr. Baldwin was responsible for planting seeds sourced from many exotic and native trees in test sites all around New Hampshire. Much experimentation was done to see which larch from different European and Asian countries would grow best here and if they could be hybridized to produce disease-resistant and fast-growing trees.

There are a large variety of pines and spruces in the Fox Forest, and larch is planted in patches throughout the property. You will also find the state champion Douglas fir and some impressive hemlocks in this forest. The hemlock and Douglas fir show how the bark on trees will change when they reach a certain age.

Start off the tour by going to the far end of the parking lot where the Tree Identification Trail goes off into the woods. Go past some red pines and Scotch pines on the way along the edge of the road. When on the trail you will see some Norway spruce and red spruce with signs on them. In just a few minutes you will come to the Douglas fir. There are several right on the trail with what looks like more off in the distance behind a stonewall. The biggest one on the trail is the state champion. It has a coarser type of bark than the trees at Woodman State Forest. Dr. Baldwin was involved in planting the trees at both these forests and others throughout the state. Look for some of the distinctive cones on the ground, and you may see some of the younger trees that have grown from the seeds.

Continue on the Tree Identification Trail past several other trees with signs until the trail meets up with the Ridge Trail. Bear left on the Ridge Trail and follow it down to the stream that runs through the property. Keep on the trail to Valley Road and then keep left on that woodland tote road up through some larch plantings and then to the dirt Concord End Road.

Burial grounds of some early residents

The best time of year to take this trip is November. That is when these larches and others you come across will have their golden yellow needles. It would be an interesting walk in the winter too, especially after a snowfall when the other evergreens have their needles covered with snow while the larches are bare in stark contrast. Check out the Gearry Cemetery at the junction with Concord End Road, then keep to the right and go across the stream and up the hill. Wander through some of the smaller larch plantings off the road on the right where you may see the many small twigs with buds that litter the ground after windstorms. Go a bit farther up the road, and just past a foundation of the old Kimball-Gearry homestead on your left you will see two European larch trees that measured the same circumference. The one away from the road is the tallest, giving it a little advantage in total points.

Start working your way back down Concord End Road to Valley Road. This time go straight on Valley Road instead of taking Ridge Trail

Old growth hemlock

at the stream. Now you are on the other side of the stream following the old road through some good-sized pines and then past a few hemlocks in the 3-foot-diameter and 100-foot-tall range. Just past the junction with Gould Pond Trail, get on Ridge Trail to the left toward Mud Pond. Don't go back to the Fox Forest headquarters until after you see the hemlock forest. Follow this narrow trail along the stream as it widens out to a small backwater pond. As you get near, the wind may calm down and you will know that a thick stand of trees is ahead. Where the trail meets Mud Pond Road you will see a sign on the left for the Virgin Forest, with magnificent hemlocks that are over 200 years old. Many of these trees are not large, but they have an old look, with very thick-ridged bark that has broken into irregular blocks. This type of bark is not often seen in most other large hemlocks. One stands out as a Big Tree that has grown very slowly over many years and looks more impressive than hemlocks at other sites that have beaten it out in size.

Difficulty rating 2

1. Douglas Fir

88" CBH   113' VH 31' ACS   Total Points 209   Excellent Condition
GPS: N 43° 08.411'   W 071° 54.820'
Δ State Champion

2. European Larch

72" CBH   98' VH   48' ACS   Total Points 182   Excellent Condition
GPS: N 43° 08.842'   W 071° 54.835'

3. Virgin Hemlock

105" CBH   109' VH 39' ACS   Total Points 224   Excellent Condition
GPS: N 43° 08.330'   W 071° 54. 336'

Directions

Take Route 9 and 202 to the Hillsborough exit and take a left on Main Street to the center of town. Turn right at the lights onto School Street, which changes to Center Road, and go about 2 miles to the Fox State Forest headquarters. Pull in and park in the dirt parking area. In November of 2013, as this book was going to press, the Fox Forest website said that the Valley Road Trail and the Concord End Road were closed due to damage from recent flooding. You should still be able to access the trees by going around the Ridge Trail past Mud Pond to the Concord End Road.

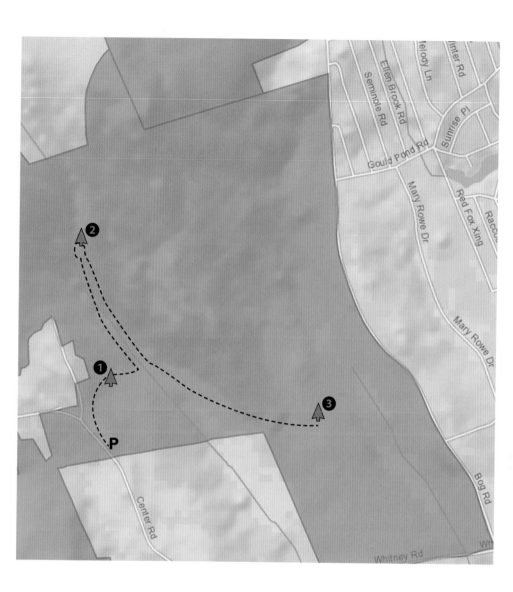

Vincent State Forest

In a remote section of Deering, you will find another state forest that has been used for the experimental testing of European species of larch, spruce, and pines. This is an opportunity to walk through some areas of larch and Norway spruce grown in close rows. This is called garden plantings, where different types of trees were planted in rows of alternate species to find out which would grow best in the same conditions. You can also find pure stands of Norway spruce that make you feel like you're in a deep, dark northern European forest—until you come out the other side and find our natural trees bringing you back to New Hampshire. The Big Trees you will find here include a European larch and a Scotch pine that are both county champions.

Walk up the trail from the road and go left after the big 150-inch-circumference oak with a stream running beside the trunk. Walk up the hillside through red pine and Scotch pine until you start seeing some Norway spruce and European larch growing on both sides of the path. Notice that some of the rows are missing where the trees that were not growing well were removed to allow the alternate rows to thrive.

Soon you will come to the Big Larch on the trail. If you are there in the winter, you may notice the golden color of the twigs at the treetop telling you that this is a European larch; the Asian versions (not found at this site) have a reddish tint to the twigs. Keep walking and you will come to another European larch about the same size where the trail turns.

There are many Scotch pines beyond a stonewall nearby. If you wander through them with your GPS, you can find the largest Scotch pine in Hillsborough County. These pines are noticeable for the pale bark on the top half of the tree, and many will look like they are winding up to the sky. This is caused by insect or bird damage to their buds as they are growing.

Winter twigs are reddish left and right on the Japanese larch and golden on the European larch in the center

I made a few forays into northern New Hampshire looking for areas with large native larch, but I found that they grew in very wet swamps, with the largest trees standing dead from insect damage. These European versions will look similar, with their golden needles in the fall and twigs that litter the ground all year. Here you will find the trees along both sides of the trail in close proximity. Keep on going up the trail and you will see a few pure stands of Norway spruce. One is on the right. Then past a culvert and up a half mile farther is a large patch that could be the focus of a longer day hike.

Quaker meeting house on the road to Vincent State Forest

Difficulty rating 2 Roads to site may be difficult to follow.

European Larch

79" CBH   105' VH 29' ACS Total Points 191 Good Condition

GPS: N 43° 06.989'   W 071° 48.480'

Δ Hillsborough Champion

Scotch Pine

64" CBH   85' VH   33' ACS Total Points 157 Excellent Condition

GPS: N 43° 07.107'   W 071° 48.819'

Δ Hillsborough Champion

Directions

From Henniker take Route 114 to Pats Peak Ski Area. Go right onto Flanders Road. Go 1.4 miles and take a left onto Gulf Road. At 1.3 miles go left on Quaker Road and follow that just over 2 miles, past the

Quaker District with its school and cemetery and past Baker Road on the right. Bear left after Dudley Pond Road and stay near Pleasant Pond to the next right (which is still Quaker Road). Continue along, with the Vincent State Forest on the left. When you come to a field and the road ends, pull over (and off the road) on the left. There is an unmarked trail going in near a stream. The parking GPS coordinates are N 43° 06.873' W 071° 48.861'.

Connecticut River Valley Oaks

I t just so happens that some of the largest oaks in New Hampshire are along the Connecticut River in Charlestown and Walpole. The river is big and the hills spring up from the valley fairly close to it in some areas. Perhaps the open area along the sides of the river allows more sunlight, which helped these oaks gain their great girth.

These trees are in neighboring towns off Route 12, a country highway that follows the New Hampshire side of the river. The trip is a pleasant drive through the valley to an old mill town and then into farm country. While in this area, be sure to stop and take a walk around the center of Walpole. It has an appealing town common, some impressive houses, and a few other good-sized trees.

Walpole town common

Walpole Mill Pond

A meandering trail beside the millpond will bring you to two oaks that you should see. The land and trail are maintained by the Walpole Conservation Commission and are examples of the New Hampshire Land and Water Conservation funds at work.

Start out at the back edge of the town cemetery and go to a sign that simply says "Pond," then walk down the trail where it directs you to go. The trail has a steep spot or two, but it is not a difficult walk. Follow the clearly seen path about half a mile, then cross a stream and walk a little farther, and keep an eye out for the first oak. It is on your right up the slope and off the trail before you get to another small stream. This is a white oak.

The property had many large white oaks at one time, but most were logged off years ago. This one was left to keep growing, perhaps as a seed tree or for the benefit of the wildlife, which is often done by those practicing good forestry methods. It also just could have had some heart rot and the logger did not think it was worth cutting.

Gnarly looking white oak

This particular tree is looking gnarly and old with a hollow center that provides a home for some animal. It appears to have engulfed a smaller tree that was growing a little too close so the older giant is just swallowing it up.

Black oak near the edge of the Walpole Mill Pond

Keep on going on the trail until you get to the edge of the millpond where a causeway once came across. The causeway is now breached and the local beaver keep reopening any attempts to repair it. You get a nice view of the small ponds that were once used by the townspeople as a water supply for an old golf course that was nearby, and to supply ice that was in much demand at the turn of the century. Look to the right, and next to the pond along the trail you will see a black oak. This tree is a good example of its species and is in excellent condition.

George Cole, a farmer, small airplane enthusiast, and sawyer who supplies wood for many boat builders, told me that the black oak is the next choice after the white oak for large boat keels. I have used it at times. It seems similar to red oak in characteristics, and it is hard to tell the difference between them in both the lumber and the living tree. The bark of the black oak is a little darker and coarser than the much more common red oak. The leaves can be smaller with deeper lobes, and the acorns have a larger cap. There is one noticeable difference, but you can tell only when cutting the tree. There is a foul odor that the freshly cut wood gives off that has encouraged the use of some unappealing nicknames for the tree. The local logger would be happy to tell you these nicknames, but you likely will not find them mentioned in many tree books.

Difficulty rating 2

White Oak

183" CBH   101' VH   79' ACS Total Points 304 Fair condition
GPS: N 43° 05.574'   W 072° 25.532'
Δ County Champion

Black Oak

150" CBH   105' VH 83' ACS Total Points 276 Excellent condition
GPS: N 43° 05.577' W 072° 25.544'
Δ County Champion

Directions

For a view of Walpole, exit Route 12 onto South Street and go to the end. Take a left onto Main Street into the center of town. Park here and walk to the town common at the end of Middle Street. Keep going around the block for a view of the town.

To see the trees, return to your car and continue north on Main Street. Bear left at the fork (which is still Main Street) and go about 0.7 miles. Just after the cemetery, turn right on North (or Cemetery) Road, then take an immediate left into another part of the cemetery. Go to the end and park. The trail sign is just off the back of the cemetery.

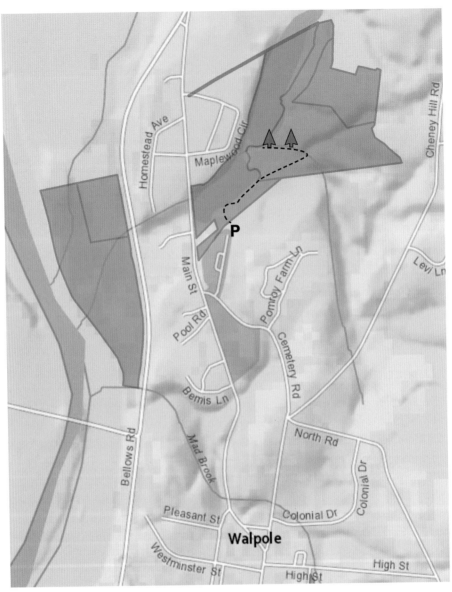

Walpole Mill Pond Oaks

Morningside Flight Park

This is your best chance to see one of the largest trees in the state that is not in someone's front yard. There are two oaks here at the top of the hill that is used as a takeoff point for hang gliders at the Morningside Flight Park. The park is privately owned, so you should check in at the office before viewing the trees. Even though there is a road up the hill, to make a hike out of it, you can park near the building and walk up to the top. The trees are right next to the road up, so you can't miss them.

Once at the top, you will have a great view of this part of the Connecticut River Valley, and on clear days can see Mount Ascutney, which is on the Vermont side of the river. If you think you need more of these views, feel free to talk to the friendly people who run the park. I am sure they will set you up with some hang gliding lessons.

Connecticut River Valley in Charlestown

Your walk is a steady uphill for about 10 to 15 minutes, and then you are there. You may have to catch your breath a few times, but it is not bad. The first tree you come to is on the right side of the road, and it is the bigger and healthier of the two. This is a red oak and is among the five largest in circumference of all types of Big Trees in the

This is an impressive red oak.

state, with the other four not readily accessible to the public. This tree is what I would call a fun tree. Although not very tall, it does have huge branches that spread out to the side, with some of them even bending down to the ground as if to beckon you to them. It will not be long before the children and even the adults will try scrambling up onto these branches.

The red oak is a common tree in my area, and in most sites where oaks are growing there will be many red oaks with a few of the other types of oaks here and there. It is used for furniture and flooring in our homes, with the poorer grade wood cut up for firewood. Red oak is a good substitute for white oak in small boats that are not moored in the water or kept out in the weather. I use it for keels, stems, and sometimes gunwales in light lapstrake canoes that are stored under cover when not in use, and it works out very well.

When ready, be sure to check out the white oak just across the road at the edge of the hill. It is an impressive tree also, listed as the second-largest white oak in the state. It does have some issues: part of the main trunk has broken off, exposing the wood to rainwater, which will rot the inside much quicker. The tree has been hanging on by sending up shoots straight into the air from the side branches. These shoots are now pretty big branches themselves, and they give the tree a different look than most.

Difficulty rating 2 Short uphill walk

Red Oak

264" CBH   55' VH   97' ACS   Total Points 343   Good Condition
GPS: N 43° 19.288'   W 072° 21.983'
Δ County Champion

White Oak

193" CBH   70' VH   78' ACS   Total Points 283   Poor Condition
GPS: N 43° 19.283'   W 072° 21.990'
Δ County Champion

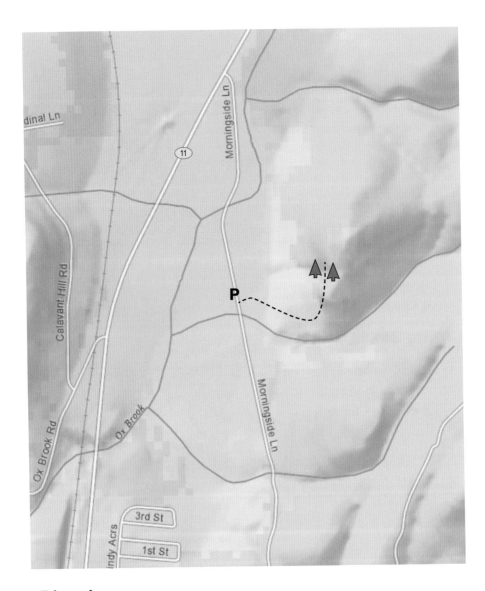

Directions

Follow Route 11/12 along the Connecticut River for 3.6 miles from Claremont (or, coming from Walpole, about 7 miles from Charlestown center). Turn onto Morningside Drive and go a little over a half-mile to Morningside Flight Park. Pull into the parking area and tell someone there that you would like to see the Big Oak trees.

Central
New Hampshire

Concord

The capitol building

Concord Tree Tour

Our capital city is not only the champion of politics in New Hampshire; it is also a leader in the number of state champion trees. This tour will bring you to an amazing variety of Big Trees that are the largest in the state and take you past others that look very impressive but have been beaten out in size by competitors in distant towns. If you need to work on your tree identification skills, then this trip will go a long way in helping you out.

It can be a walking tour or a bike tour. If biking, expect frequent stops because there are short distances between most of the trees. If walking, it may be better to walk to the trees near the center of town, then drive to a few that are on the southern outskirts, some distance away, although they all could be walked to if you like.

There are plenty of others things to see in downtown Concord, such as the capitol buildings, and the state office park, which hosts many of the trees. You are sure to want to stop for lunch at Cheers or one of the other local restaurants and do some antique shopping if time allows. We were lucky enough to catch a Greek festival and picked up some delicious baklava dessert, then walked through an arts fair in the central plaza.

Start the tour at the southern end of town, where you can park your car next to Rollins Park and view the Siberian elm that is across the street. These were planted extensively after the Dutch elm disease started killing off most of the American elms. The leaves of Siberian elm are much smaller, and the wood is brittle, which makes the tree prone to storm damage.

Go up Broadway and take a right on Pillsbury Street to an American elm that has survived. It is close to the building on the South Main Street side of New Hampshire Public Radio. American elms were once planted in cities all across the United States. The lumber has a reputation as being slow to decompose when in contact with water, so it was commonly used for gutters on houses. The old underground sewer pipes from the eighteenth century that were dug up in Portsmouth were made of elm. I have used it when steam bending difficult bends for frames in larger wood boat repairs.

Continue on to South Main Street and take a left at the fork for South State Street. Just after the first building down on the left you will see an osage orange tree. (It is on private property, so just view it from the sidewalk.)

These were extensively used in the Great Plains as hedgerows to keep domestic animals from wandering off. When planted close together and trimmed, their thorny branches weave together in an impenetrable barrier to livestock. Named after the Osage tribe, the wood of this tree has been used for making hunting bows since the Native Americans roamed the land. The large lime-colored fruits are loved by squirrels but have been known to be a choking hazard for cows and horses who try to swallow them whole.

From here cut across town about twelve blocks to the old New Hampshire Hospital grounds. The total walking distance for the whole tour will be about four miles. If you want a shorter walk, you could start the tour by driving to view the first three trees then park at the hospital grounds to see the rest, shaving about 1.5 miles off the walking distance. If walking or biking the whole distance keep going up South State Street to West Street and go about eight blocks to Broadway and onto Clinton Street. Continue to the grounds entrance just past the Concord District Courthouse.

Once in the entrance, follow the outer road to the right around the parking lot near the lawn until you come to a small pedestrian bridge over a small creek. Then walk quite a ways across the lawn to see the honey locust. This species has long seed pods and 18 to 28 leaflets on a stem. Some varieties have thorns and some do not. The lumber is well known as long lasting when in contact with the soil and is sought after for fence posts and framing for wooden boats. Although it is not a very large tree for its type, it is good sized and has unusual features that will add to your tree identification skills. Now continue to the end of the lawn area to the back of the buildings at Dollof Square to a large pin oak. You can tell this by its long bristles, or pins, on the end of its leaves and its distinctive crown shape. This stands out as quite a tall tree.

Slippery elm on Orchard Street

Go left and through the parking lots up to Short Street and bear right until you are in front of the buildings near the Department of Labor. Here you will see three European beech trees in close proximity that are worth checking out. Then continue northwest on the main road to the flowering dogwood in front of the main building. This building was the original New Hampshire Asylum, which was expanded to include the campus all around you. The state housed up to 2700 mentally challenged individuals here in the 1950's. A national push to deinstitutionalize these patients led to empty buildings and the state now uses them as office space. The beautiful spring flowers on this dogwood must have offered at least some peace to those that lived here. Cut across the front of the campus toward the lawn area on Wheelock Drive. Go past some large oaks and around to the left toward the front exit, where on the right you will see the state co-champion Norway spruce and a double-trunked hemlock that is the Merrimack county champion.

Once out of the grounds, cross the street and go left on the main road, Route 9, and take the first right onto Pine Street and then a right onto Orchard. About halfway down you will see your third species of elm on this tour, the slippery elm, which you can't miss at 125 inches in circumference. I have had occasion to use lumber from this species of tree for the ribs in my canoes. The wood is lightweight, bends easily, and has very stringy grain that resists cracking. It is not readily available at the local sawmills and ash is a good substitute, so I use that more often. Slippery elm is named for its slippery inner bark that is known for its medicinal uses and is chewed to relieve sore throats.

At the end of Orchard Street go left on Merrimac and then take the first right onto Warren to the corner of Warren and Rumford. In the backyard of the corner house behind the fence, you will see a European beech along with a large yellow poplar, also known as tuliptree, which has distinctive four-lobed leaves and tulip-like flowers. These are on private property, so just view them from the sidewalk. Then continue on down Warren to the second left on Green Street and you will see two unusual curling American smoketrees in front of the Concord Housing and Redevelopment building. They are found growing naturally in the southern United States and are known for their vibrant colored leaves in the fall. The tree is named for the smoky gray look of the spring flowers. The largest one here is tied for the national champion for the type.

Go on to Capitol Street and go right to the main drag where the downtown stores are. You may want to think about stopping for lunch about now. You could get a sandwich to go, then have a relaxing lunch at the central plaza or eat in at your choice of several downtown restaurants.

When ready, make your way back to the Capitol Building. Right in front next to the entrance you cannot miss the large Norway maple. Once planted in many cities and parks, it is no longer widely used because it spreads like wildfire and takes over where native species would otherwise grow. Wander across to the church on the left and you will see an American larch, or tamarack, next to it. Hackmatack is also a common name for this species in Maine and New Hampshire, and I like to use that name. This is a long-lasting wood that is excellent for use as knees for stems and bracing in small boats. This specimen is big for its type, as many in their natural settings die of diseases brought on by insects before reaching this size. This tree and the Norway maple are current state champions.

Now to finish this tour, go behind the capitol to North State Street and go all the way to the circle at Franklin Street. Use the crosswalk on the right and look at the tuliptree next to the house on the right. Stay on the sidewalk while viewing this tree. Then go on to the next right (Church Street) and go to the end at the traffic lights where Route 202 and Route 3 meet. Be very careful crossing here, and be sure to push the walk button to get across. Watch out that no one runs the light. Another option would be to keep going on North State Street and cross Route 3 at the end where they meet and then go down to N. Main Street and the sycamore.

The final tree on this tour is well worth seeing, so do not miss it. This is the state's largest American sycamore and is impressive. The sycamores are natural to the Eastern United States and are more common near our rivers down south. In New Hampshire they are found most times in an urban setting like this. It is distinctive with its large trunk and whitish upper limbs. This species has the largest trunks of any American hardwood. The current national champion has a diameter of over 11 feet.

American sycamore

Difficulty rating 2   Some distance to see them all

1. Siberian Elm

132" CBH   85' VH   64' ACS   Total Points 233   Excellent Condition

GPS: N 43° 11.164'   W 071° 32.075'

Δ **County Champion**

2. American Elm

131" CBH   75' VH   81' ACS   Total Points 226   Excellent Condition

GPS: N 43° 11.540'   W 071° 31.987'

Δ **County Champion**

3. Osage Orange

131" CBH   58' VH   56' ACS   Total Points 203   Good Condition

GPS: N 43° 11.651'   W 071° 31.920'

Δ **State Champion**

4. Honey Locust

120" CBH   90' VH   82' ACS   Total Points 231 Excellent Condition
GPS: N 43° 11.785'   W 071° 32.479'
Δ State Champion

5. Pin Oak

135" CBH   82' VH   87' ACS   Total Points 239 Excellent Condition
GPS: N 43° 11.820'   W 071° 32.547'
Δ County Champion

6. European Beech

140" CBH   70' VH   64' ACS   Total Points 226 Excellent Condition
GPS: N 43° 11.893'   W 071° 32.598'

7. Flowering Dogwood

40" CBH   78' VH   28' ACS   Total Points 125 Excellent Condition
GPS: N 43° 11.919'   W 071° 32.675'
Δ State Champion

8. Norway Spruce

169" CBH   82' VH   56' ACS   Total Points 265 Excellent Condition
GPS: N 43° 12.027'   W 071° 32.316'
Δ State Co-Champion

9. Eastern Hemlock

148" CBH   79' VH   68' ACS   Total Points 244 Excellent Condition
GPS: N 43° 12.033'   W 071° 32.589'
Δ County Champion

10. Slippery Elm

125" CBH   81' VH   66' ACS   Total Points 223 Good Condition
GPS: N 43° 12.099'   W 071° 32.654'
Δ State Champion

11. European Beech

178" CBH   102' VH 65' ACS   Total Points 296 Good Condition
GPS: N 43° 12.181'   W 071° 32.536'

Δ County Champion

12. Tuliptree

138" CBH   116' VH 79' ACS   Total Points 274 Good Condition
GPS: N 43° 12.792'   W 071° 32.500'

Δ County Champion

13. American Smoketree

96" CBH   50' VH   34' ACS   Total Points 155 Excellent Condition
GPS: N 43° 12.294'   W 071° 32.373'

Δ National Champion

14. Norway Maple

154" CBH   68' VH   73' ACS   Total Points 240 Good Condition
GPS: N 43° 12.437   W 071° 32.224'

Δ State Champion

15. Tamarack

102" CBH   80' VH   48' ACS   Total Points 194 Good Condition
GPS: N 43° 12.456'   W 071° 32.288'

Δ State Champion

16. American Sycamore

209" CBH   106' VH 119' ACS   Total Points 345   Fair Condition
GPS: N 43° 12.897'   W 071° 32.455'

State Champion

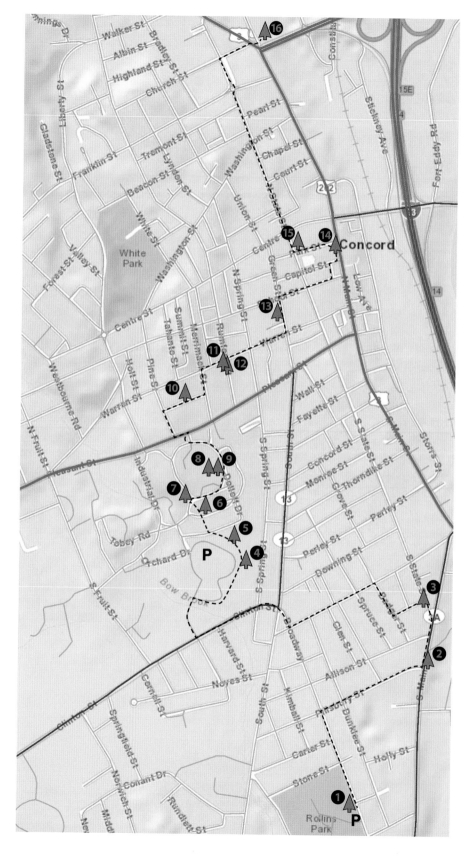

Pitch Pine

Pinus rigida

White Lake State Park is a great place to camp overnight with young children or just to spend the day. It has those clean white beaches we all love, and with Mount Chocorua in the background, the scenery can't be beat. This part of New Hampshire has the sandy soil that the pitch pine thrives in, with a few of the largest forests of this type of pine spreading from here and into Maine. The lakes of the area, including White Lake, Ossipee Lake, and Square Pond, all have the same clean-looking pure white sand. You could visit here in the summer for swimming and hiking with the crowds or wait till the off-season of late fall or winter. There is a nice playground that may be hard to get the kids away from, but once you get them going they will enjoy the trail around the lake.

Take the trail out to the left from the playground and beach area and follow it along the lakeshore. There are some fair-sized white pines and pitch pines spread throughout. About half a mile down the path you will find the tree on the left. It has been beat out for the county champ but is large enough to show you what the big pitch pines are like. It is a nice, straight, clear-trunked example, with bark that is neat to look at and seems to fit right into the landscape. New Hampshire has the national champion of this species that is on private land in the western part of the state.

White Lake with Mount Chocorua

The pitch pine is used for construction lumber but was well known for the use of its sap and turpentine as "naval stores" for a resin base in building and maintaining wooden ships. The pine tar that I have used is mixed with linseed oil to make a traditional deck oil that is easy to apply.

When checking the tree I wondered what kind of wildlife could be associated with it, but I did not see anything around. After about ten minutes I could hear loons calling farther up the lake. Then some mergansers started circling right near the shore by me, and finally a mature bald eagle flew by and was eyeing the mergansers. I guess I will choose the bald eagle because it was impressive to see and also would likely have more use for the tall pines for roosting.

After viewing the tree, you could continue on the trail to circum-navigate the lake. There are some side trails that will take you to a black spruce bog, which would be interesting to see.

Pitch pine at White Lake State Park

Difficulty rating 1

103" CBH   99' VH   28' ACS   Total points 209   Excellent condition
GPS: N 43° 50.170'   W 071° 13.438'

Directions

This site is easy to get to. Just look for the sign for White Lake State
Park off Route 16 in West Ossipee just past the junction of Route 25
and Route 41. Pull into the parking area by the beach and take the trail
to the left that follows the lakeshore. The tree is less than ½ mile from
the beach on the left.

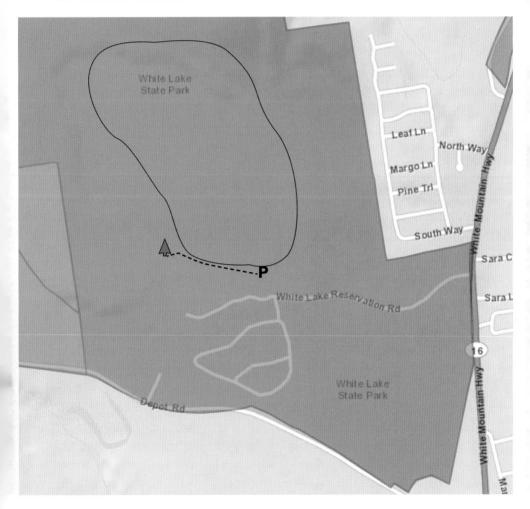

Butternut

Juglans cinerea L.

The trip to see this "white walnut" will bring you into one of the best parts of New Hampshire. The small mountains are beautiful, and Squam Lake is thought by many to be the best large lake in the state. This area is not overdeveloped like other nearby vacation spots and gives the true outdoor experience when you are hiking or boating. The town of Center Sandwich has a few small shops along with the town churches and public buildings, all attired in their distinctive white paint. Add to that a cluster of New England and Cape-style homes and you have what seems like the perfect small town setting.

Things are not quite so perfect with the butternut tree species, though, as it is under attack by a fungus that is killing them throughout their range. This is a fairly new problem that was imported into this country in the 1960s and in the last twenty years or so has quickly spread to most of the trees in New Hampshire. Attempts are being made to grow nursery stock grafted from the shoots and buds of disease-resistant trees and transplant them into the woods. Only time will tell if the butternut trees in this state will come back.

To see this tree you will walk down the scenic Sandwich Notch Road, which goes for 8.5 miles through the Sandwich Mountains and out to Route 49 in Thornton. This road had as many as three hundred homes on it at one time. It was maintained as an important trade route so farmers could bring their produce from northern New Hampshire and Vermont through the mountains to the big towns of Portsmouth, New Hampshire, and Portland, Maine.

For an addition to this trip to the butternut tree, you could keep walking on the notch road about a mile from your car, and just above the first bridge on your right you will see Pulpit Rock, where the local preacher used to hold services for the townspeople in the early 1800s. They preferred to worship here rather than at the meetinghouse in

This butternut is growing at the site of an old homestead.

town. There is also much more to see off other nearby trails if you want to wander farther down the road.

On the way to the butternut there is a bigtooth aspen on the right just over the stonewall. Called poplar by most locals, this is a prime example and it has one of the larger circumferences for this species in the state. Keep going up to where the land levels out and you will see stone foundations and stonewalls all around. The butternut tree is right in the middle of one of the stonewalls and stands out among all other trees in the area.

This species has compound leaves with eleven to seventeen leaflets. The fruit is a nut enclosed by a sticky haired husk. American Indians used the oil from the nuts to make a type of butter, which led to the name of butternut.

This wood and canvas canoe built by the author has butternut decks and gunwales.

The lumber is especially light in weight, with grain similar to that of mahogany but in a blonde color. It is occasionally used for furniture and will take a high polish and finish nicely. The cost of the premium lumber has taken off recently because it is getting rare and the wood is often of poor quality from the fungus. I have used it for decks and gunwales on the canoes for a nice contrast with a dark-colored paint on the canvas.

Sandwich Mountains

Difficulty rating 2

Big Tooth Aspen

81" CBH   95' VH   46' ACS   Total Points 188   Good Condition
GPS: N 43° 49.346'   W 071° 29.416'

Butternut

132" CBH   109' VH 59' ACS   Total Points 256   Fair Condition
GPS: N 43° 49.356'   W 071° 29.484'
Δ County Champion

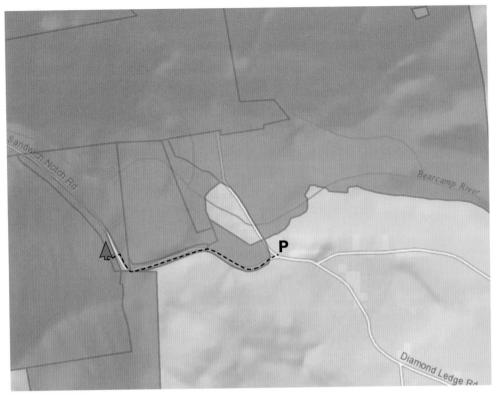

Butternut on Sandwich Notch Road

Directions

In Center Sandwich where Route 113 meets Route 109, take Grove Street north (it changes its name to Diamond Ledge Road). Go a little over 2 miles and there is a parking area on the left where Sandwich Notch Road begins. Some of the road can be driven in the summer, but it can be rough and you should park here and walk in. At ½ mile from the parking area the road takes a sharp turn, and you will go up the rutted woods road on the left to the tree. This was at one time the driveway to the old homestead where the butternut is located.

White Oak
Quercus alba

T raveling to this oak will give you a good look at a variety of ter-
rain with a farm field and power line bordering a state forest.
A small brook runs near the tree and empties into the Turkey
River at the far end of the property. This is just outside the city of Concord in the Cilley State Forest, where the short walk will be a welcome
escape for the people living in this more urban area.

The white oak is thought to be the best of the oak types in the
Northeast because it has better burning value for firewood and is more
durable. In my boatbuilding experience, it is sought out for the keels
and frames of boats small and large as it lasts longer, is stronger, and
resists cracking or breaking better than other oaks. If in healthy condition, it is the more handsome tree with nice bark and rounder-edged
leaves. The acorns are even more appealing. If you hand split a bolt of
white oak, you will notice that it does not just jump apart when hit
with a maul. The fibers of the wood try to hold together, and you often
have to force it apart with more maul strikes or pull it apart with your
hands. The wood was used for many farm implements and is the preferred wood for whiskey barrels because it will not readily absorb the
whiskey into the wood. It also bends easily. I once put ribs in a Rangeley
Lake Boat by using "green" (freshly cut) white oak, which bent right in
without steaming.

A nice example of a big white oak

I would suggest spending some time on your own around this tree and some of the others in this book. With no other distractions you can really look around and appreciate what is right in front of you. The trunk of this tree where the rain splashes up on it is growing its own small garden of moss. Small animals may live in the crevices around the trunk, and strange-looking mushrooms may be sprouting up. Check out its size and bark quality from all sides. Be sure to check over the tree's health to see what has happened over the years and if there are any major problems such as bark that is falling off or large dead branches where rot may start. Step back and look at its height and notice how the nearby trees are affected. Some may be dying from its shade while others seem to be waiting in its shadow for the chance to sprout up at the loss of a large branch or if a windstorm takes out this bigger neighbor. What was the history of the tree in the prospective of the land around it? What happened to make it so big compared to its neighbors? Many large trees are near a source of water. Do the roots of this tree reach all the way to the small brook? The brook adds to the appeal, so be sure to take it all in. What is growing near the brook and how does the tree affect it? You may not get all the answers, but you could take the time to contemplate all these questions and more while visiting these Big Trees of New Hampshire.

Be sure to check out all around the bottom of these Big Trees. You never know what you will discover.

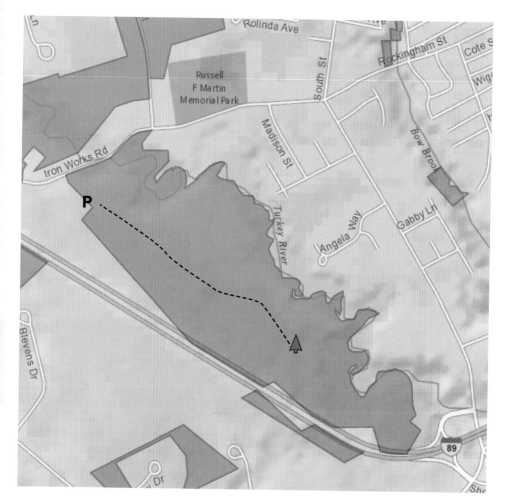

Difficulty rating 2

173" CBH   96' VH   75' ACS   Total Points 288   Fair Condition

GPS: N 43° 10.330'   W 71° 32.573'

Δ County Co-Champion

Directions

Take I-89 to exit 2 onto Route 13 (Clinton Street) toward Concord. Take the first right on Iron Works Road. Go about half a mile and take a right onto a small dirt road near a house. Follow it down and park near a gated access road into the woods.

About the Author

K evin Martin has been interested in working with wood all of his adult life. His interest was brought on by his father's collection of woodworking tools and the wooden boat that his father had built. Early on Kevin put in a four-year apprenticeship as a union carpenter before starting his own business. For over thirty-three years he has carried on the tradition of boatbuilding by building well over one hundred small crafts and restoring many more. A visit to his workshop will usually yield at least one or two fascinating canoes or boats in progress.

His interest in working with wood has led him to admire the giant trees he comes across as he travels the woods of New Hampshire. At first he looked at them as prime sources of good lumber for his work. After serving many years on the town Conservation Commission, and then the Lamprey River Advisory Committee he has since learned of their many other important benefits. Kevin's interest in Big Trees began when searching for some trees he had heard about in the wildlife studies that were completed along the Lamprey River. He found some state champions in special natural settings, which brought about a great respect for the different types of forests found in New Hampshire.

Kevin and his wife, Kim, have raised a family of four children in the house that they built in Epping on the banks of the Lamprey River. They now have 8 grandchildren that visit often and go along with him in the woods. He is an accomplished naturalist and outdoorsman, and shares many of his experiences in *Big Trees of New Hampshire*.

Index by Tree Type